In Search of Joseph

In Search of Joseph

Shannon M. Tracy

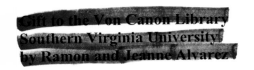
KenningHouse

Dedication

This book is humbly dedicated to my wife, Vicki, and our five children—
Christopher, Benjamin, Spencer, Alison, and Sterling—
from whom I receive my greatest joy,
for all the long nights and days I have spent away from them working on this project.

Images on pages 8, 10, 11, 12, 21, and 27 left are used by permission of the Church Museum of LDS History and Art.

© Copyright 1995 Shannon M. Tracy
Published by KenningHouse
1087 East 680 North
Orem, Utah 84057

ISBN: 1-57636-005-9
Library of Congress Catalog Number: 95-72029

Printed by Precision Litho
Design by Cairo Design Group

Contents

Chapter 4
Joseph, the Man
20

Chapter 5
An Unexpected Discovery
24

Chapter 6
"To Seal the Testimony": Death Comes to Carthage
26

Chapter 7
The Search for the Unknown Grave
34

Chapter 8
Forensic Evidence: A Closer Look
48

Chapter 9
Putting It All Together
62

Contents

Acknowledgments

In the truest sense, this project was a team effort. From the very beginning the complexities demanded the assembling of a group of experts. Each brought to the project his or her unique abilities. Knowing in advance that listing those who deserve acknowledgment and thanks is dangerous at best, I would be remiss in not making the attempt.

First thanks goes to my greatest fan and my best support—my wife, Vicki. Her faith in me let us divert family funds to this project, therefore postponing building our home. This sacrifice of course was shared by my five children.

My heartfelt thanks goes to my parents who provided a home environment that allowed me to explore and pursue my interests—including those that led to a deep, early love for the Prophet Joseph.

Special thanks goes to Dr. Kent Van De Graaff, Brigham Young University professor emeritus of human anatomy, and Dr. Niles Herrod, a prominent Provo maxillofacial surgeon, for their expertise, counsel, and advice.

This project would have been impossible without the skills of Chris Creek and the "crew" (Roger Clarke and Eric Merritt) at Zygote Media.

My graditude is extended to Eldred G. Smith, Patriarch Emeritus to The Church of Jesus Christ of Latter-day Saints, for his generosity in allowing our team the privilege of viewing, measuring, and photographing Hyrum Smith's clothing and other personal effects.

My sincere appreciation is given to Glen Leonard, director of the Church Museum of LDS History and Art for accommodating my first request, which allowed me to launch this incredible journey.

Ronald Romig, archivist for the Reorganized Church of Jesus Christ of Latter Day Saints, has my special gratitude for early-on and continuing support. It was he who offered help in obtaining

permission to publish the rare photographs of the brothers.

Finally, special acknowledgment needs to be given to my editorial and production team members: Ted Gibbons, who was my research and content editor, providing knowledge and background of and insight into Joseph and Hyrum; Linda Hunter Adams, my technical editor; Jane Clayson, the typesetter and production editor; Douglass and Peggy Cole of the Cairo Design Group, who designed the cover and text of the book; Bruce Stone, who brought together all the elements at the press; and Larry Barkdull at *KenningHouse*, who believed.

In Search of Joseph

CHAPTER 1

"Sir, I Would See Joseph"

It was September of 1823. James Monroe and his wife Elizabeth had been in the White House since 1817. In three months the Monroe Doctrine would warn the nations of Europe not to interfere in the Western Hemisphere. The Erie Canal was under construction but two years from completion, its progress encouraged by Governor De Witt Clinton of New York. With the consent of Mexico, settlers were swarming to Texas. Jacksonville, Florida, was a year old. Los Angeles was twenty-seven years from incorporation. A year earlier, Brazil had declared herself independent from Portugal, and in January, the United States had formally recognized Argentina and Chile. Gas streetlights were burning for the first time in New Orleans. Dr. Edwin James had recently used the term "great desert" to describe Wyoming, and James Fenimore Cooper had just published the first of the *Leatherstocking Tales*.

Portentous events were shaping and reshaping the world, and periodicals proclaimed the most significant of them in bold-face type and colossal fonts.

But that September something else was happening—an event whose significance so far eclipsed all others that they would, in the light of untarnished truth and millennial glory, be forever lost in the shadows of secular confusion.

In Manchester Township in northwest New York, God was shaping a prophet.

The prophetic call had come earlier, in the spring of 1820, when a boy named Joseph Smith had experienced a theophany whose like had not been reported since the stoning of Stephen. It was now time for the preparation to proceed. On the evening of the twenty-first

2

of September, Joseph retired to "[his] bed" in "[his] room." Joseph shared his home with five brothers and three sisters, but the sense of his report is that he was alone. A new home was under construction, the project directed by the oldest of the Smith boys, Alvin. But the desperate need for room had impelled the family to move to the unfinished structure the spring before. It was in this residence that Joseph's instruction continued.

The three-and-one-half years since that initial contact with Deity had been a time of testing for the lad. His awareness of a call to an extraordinary mission accompanied him much of the time, but his youthful exuberance and cheerful nature were a concern to him, for they occasionally led him into activities which he felt, because of his call, he ought to have avoided. So, this night, he prayed. Alone in the room with his guilt and his longing, he poured out his soul in supplication for

forgiveness and divine confirmation that he remained serviceable to the Lord.

An angel came. Joseph said he prayed with full confidence that a manifestation would come, and he was right. The increasing light attending this celestial minister

The Smith home in Palmyra where Joseph was visited by the angel Moroni

must have evoked sudden memories of the light in the grove where Joseph had seen God the Father and his Son Jesus Christ. On the night of September 21, the intensity of the illumination grew until the room was more radiant than at midday.

The wonder and power of the event frightened him, but only for a moment. He had prayed for this and his prayer had been answered. This glorious being introduced himself as Moroni, a "messenger sent from the presence of God" to Joseph. The boy must have rejoiced in the announcement that God *still* had a work for him to do.

And then, at the beginning of a prophetic description of part of the work that Joseph would be called to do, and before giving a scriptural portrait of events related to the last days, this heavenly being uttered a prophecy—a prophecy of so unlikely a nature and improbable a fulfillment that even at the distance of a century and a half we wonder at the foreknowledge necessary to speak it, and the courage required to write it.

"Your name," Moroni prophesied, "will be had for good and evil among all nations, kindreds, and tongues. It will be both good and evil spoken of among all people."

Joseph was less than three months from his eighteenth birthday. He had, in the years of his life, lived in Vermont, New Hampshire, and New York, always on small farms associated with insignificant villages. We know of only one famous person that he had met in those years: Doctor Nathan Smith of Dartmouth College, who operated on Joseph's leg for osteomyelitis when Joseph was eight years old. Joseph's schooling had occupied a portion of three years of his life. His noteworthy skills may have included modest farming ability, some experience at construction, some competence at sums and reading, and a love for and confidence in the Bible. New York was the third state in which he had lived, but even in Palmyra he was less than three hundred miles from the small Sharon farmhouse where he was born.

Of course others have risen from insignificant origins to international fame. Most of these have had either good or evil spoken of them, but rarely both with such passion as has had Joseph Smith. And which of them had the temerity to predict

so unlikely an outcome so far in advance of its fulfillment. Which of them, in an upper room of an uncompleted farmhouse in an unremarkable township in an uncelebrated county on the frontier of New York, predicted such a happening to the world?

Joseph was arrested forty times, the charges against him sworn by people infuriated by his teachings. The outrage continues. When the LDS temple was dedicated in Chicago, anti-Mormons filled the sidewalk in front of the building, giving away armloads of derogatory and inflammatory materials produced to deprecate the work of Joseph Smith. And yet, on every continent, congregations of the faithful sing with absolute assurance of this same man, "Praise to the man who communed with Jehovah. Jesus anointed that prophet and seer!"

Perhaps the very controversy furthers the cause. It is impossible to be indifferent about a man who claimed to have conversed with the Father and the Son, a man who declared all Christian creeds apostate, a man who produced a volume of sacred literature that is more widely distributed than any other book on earth except the Bible. What sort of man could have caused so enormous a diversity of opinion?

This is the kind of controversy Jesus caused with his miracles and his teachings and his affirmations of divine authority. Such claims drew the honest in heart from both the first and the nineteenth centuries, with their longing for truth and light. They came from the farms and the schools, from the city and the country. They came seeking, hoping, praying. They came as the Greeks came to Philip in John 12, saying "Sir, we would see Jesus."

I understand the yearning behind the request of those Greeks. The accounts of the achievements of the Prophet from Palmyra have forged in me a similar passion. I have desired to walk down Mulholland Street in Nauvoo, to meet his brother Hyrum at the gate of the Mansion House, and to say to him, "Sir, I would see Joseph."

Of course I was not searching for a face at first, but for a character. I wanted to comprehend the essence of this remarkable man. I wanted to rejoice in the reality of his prophetic power. I wanted to stand with him next to the open curtains of heaven and, for the briefest instant, to peer within.

That yearning has taken me on a journey. The paths I have followed have not led me to the anticipated destinations. Often they have curved into unexpected territories. But those paths have, finally, brought me face to face with Joseph Smith. I have, in the midst of a journey to *know* Joseph, found myself in a place where I have also been able to *see* him. This is the story of that journey.

CHAPTER 2

Worm Tracks and Computers

y brother is a deputy sheriff. He wears a gun and enforces the law. He and I grew up together in the same home; we listened to the same bedtime stories and watched the same television programs. Our parents cherished us and nurtured us and taught us many of the same things. My inclinations, perhaps flowing from some premortal propensity, have taken me in a different direction. The focus of my life has been in electronics.

When I was eight I broke my right arm and as a result fell dangerously behind in my penmanship. My teacher confronted me. She told me that my penmanship looked like worm tracks in wet dirt, and she made it clear that I needed more discipline and more practice in order to bring my skills back to the level of my class. With a boldness I cannot now comprehend, and with a foresight I do not understand, I told her that some day when I got older I would have a machine that would write for me and I would have no need for penmanship. Practice for me was, therefore, a waste of time.

She was not entertained by my rebellion. "Typewriters," she informed me imperiously, "will never replace handwriting!" The teacher was right twice that day. My handwriting still looks like worm tracks, and typewriters did not replace handwriting. But years passed and converging lines of inspired technology made it possible for me to acquire my first personal computer. This extraordinary device wrote legibly for me, and then checked my spelling. I hope Mrs. Weeks has been watching. The personal computer did more, however, than prove me prophetic to a third-grade teacher. I have owned several computers, and I now know that using a computer only for word-processing is like using a Ferrari as a taxi. The computer opened doors to invisible worlds and made it possible for me to go to unimaginable places and to do impossible things.

Computer technology and innovative programs can do more than re-create reality. Impossible, previously incomprehensible creations are now a matter of a few keystrokes. Inanimate objects can be assembled in three dimensions, and then they can be made to move, to change, to grow, even to speak.

Operators use computers to search the knowledge of remote libraries. They download games and stories and electronic magazines. They review pictures of the planets of the solar system and the mites that inhabit human eyebrows. And new doors swing open with mind-boggling rapidity, offering glimpses of new dimensions of discovery. All of this fascinates me, and I wish I had the time and equipment to explore every new avenue that opens. But my greatest interest is three-dimensional (3-D) animation. It became an obsession. I immersed myself in this new technology, and my affection and my competence increased.

Throughout the years of this technological revolution, I continued to study Joseph

Early etching of Joseph

Smith. My regard for him intensified as I read the biography his mother wrote, then others his followers had penned. As I matured, I became aware of the negative voices—the *evil-speakers*—who had written their convoluted and irreconcilable histories. I was saddened that in their quest to destroy him, they should drag themselves so far from him. The following statement by Governor Thomas Ford of Illinois is typical of attacks by Joseph's detractors:

"Joseph Smith was the most successful imposter in modern times: a man who though ignorant and coarse, had some great natural parts, which fitted him for temporary success, but which were so obscured and counteracted by the inherent corruption and vices of his nature that he never could succeed in establishing a system of policy which looked to permanent success in the future."[1]

I had never expected that Joseph Smith was perfect, but I knew from my own searching that he was not "ignorant and coarse" nor filled with the "inherent corruption and vices" described by so many.

I searched for and examined the images that had been made of him. Some were clearly well done and nearly photographic, their artistic execution gratifying. Others were more stylized and imaginative. But even in the renditions of the paintings for which Joseph himself might have posed—images which were presented as true likenesses—I encountered enormous variety. I compared some of these works and wondered if they were of the same man. The results of this review were frustrating. I often asked myself, "What did he really look like? Which of these many images is correct?"

This man had commanded a legion of five thousand soldiers. He built from the swamps the largest city in Illinois. He announced himself a candidate for the Presidency of the United States. He wrote books of revelation, doctrine, and prophecy. I just wanted to know what he looked like.

I knew what Brigham looked like, and John Taylor and Lorenzo Snow, but not Joseph.

As I studied more about Joseph and his life, I also came to better appreciate his brother Hyrum, with his selfless dedication to his younger brother and to the cause of Christ. But, once again, I could not find any definitive description of Hyrum, and nothing at all that could be accepted as a reliable image.

I finally determined that I would never see the actual likenesses of these men on this mortal earth. And so, with the other impossible and unfulfilled dreams of my youth, I consigned this one to the dusty back shelves in my mind, and got on with my life.

The ideas and dreams in my head had never been expressed, due to my lack of artistic coordination. I was never one who could take pen or brush in hand and create something that others would find enjoyable.

But now, with a good paint package and a Computer Aided Design (CAD) program, I could re-create reality and then accomplish things that were impossible to do in the real world. I discovered software packages that could provide a format for personal expression and give an output close to perfection. The chains were broken. With a computer and the right software packages, I was free to create according to the inclinations of my heart and to the extent of my ability.

As I immersed myself in this new technology, and as my affection and ability increased, I continued to examine that old but enduring dream on one of those dusty

back shelves in my mind. I wanted to see Joseph Smith.

It was with the background of these interests in three-dimensional animation and the Prophet Joseph Smith that I visited a special exhibit on Joseph and Hyrum Smith at the Museum of LDS History and Art in the fall of 1994. Again, as in the past, I looked upon the many images of the brothers. I saw such diversity, and the old questions surfaced again. If I were to meet him at the temple in Kirtland, would I recognize him? Were there enough similarities in these portraits to identify the man in person?

It was at that moment that it happened. In an unexpected convergence of interest and opportunity, I found myself standing before the case that contained the death masks of the Prophet Joseph and his brother Hyrum. George Cannon, father of George Q.

Cannon, had assisted in preparing the bodies of the Martyrs when they were returned to Nauvoo from Carthage. He was one of only a handful of men in Nauvoo who had a knowledge of the process of making death masks. Sometime on the twenty-eighth of July, between the arrival of the bodies in Nauvoo at about 3:00 p.m. and the inception of the viewing that evening at about 6:00 p.m., he made plaster casts of the faces of the slain brothers. Copies of those masks now lay before me.

There was a soft yellow light playing upon them, and they were brown with age, a network of small cracks attesting to the continuous handling they had received. I regarded them with reverent awe. I knew that at that moment I was seeing the actual features of these great men. None of the questions surrounding the paintings and drawings applied to these objects. The actual features of their faces lay before me, and I had the foreboding, standing there, that this might be as close as I would ever come to seeing them.

I paused a moment, examining the facial contours depicted by the masks, trying to imagine them enclosed in flesh. Then, in the solemnity of that moment, a thought transfixed me: *I wonder why no one has ever digitized into a computer the death masks of these two great men and then made correct likenesses of them from a 3-D model?*

It could be done. I knew that the genuine features of their faces lay before me. The color and form of the masks made it difficult to imagine them as faces of flesh and blood, but with the computer technology I used, and access to the masks themselves, such lifelike images could be constructed! Some parts of the process might require skills beyond my own, but I knew I could put together a team of experts to do it. Why hadn't someone else done this?

This connection of computer technology and the death masks seemed so logical and practical that I at once assumed that a 3-D model had not been made because it must be impossible to get permission to use the masks for such a purpose. Joseph and Hyrum Smith were men of international reputation! It was inconceivable to me that no one had

Early etching of Hyrum

ever suggested such a project before, and I walked away with some sadness, trying to envision what the results of such a study might be.

I tried to set the idea aside, but I could not suppress it. Again and again the questions forced themselves to the forefront of my thoughts. "What if it has just never been attempted?" I kept wondering. "What if no one has ever asked for permission to undertake such a project?"

During the next several days I discussed the idea with colleagues and, without real hope, considered the equipment and technology that would be required to make correct, lifelike images of the two brothers.

Once the masks were digitized three-dimensionally into the computer, only the first part of the enterprise would be completed. I would need an anatomist to examine the images and suggest adjustments, if any, that might be necessary to correct the likenesses. I would need to review all the recorded facts about the appearances of the brothers and integrate pertinent information about the injuries they suffered at the time of their deaths. An anatomist could assist me in locating a skull that

One of the few images of Hyrum by Maudsley

would conform as closely as possible to the available information conveyed by the death masks about these men. This procedure would make it possible to complete a truly lifelike image, not just of the face, but of the entire head. With such information, I could portray the Prophet's actual appearance with exceptional accuracy.

It could all be done!

Only one obstacle prevented it from happening: I did not have access to the death masks.

I tried again to forget, but I could not. My mind would not give up on it. I had to know. So, as it is my nature to start at the top, I called the Church Museum and asked for the person who was in charge there. I was given the name of Glen Leonard and his phone number. With great anticipation, I dialed the number.

"Hello, this is Glen Leonard." The voice was comfortable and friendly. These few words and his tone of voice convinced me that I had found someone who would listen and at least give me the chance to share what was in my mind. I hesitated for a moment, then plunged right in and began to explain what it was I wanted to do and a little of how I would be able to accomplish it. Glen was an expert on the images of Joseph and had devoted significant time to the analysis of those images and so my proposal interested him. He recommended that I put my request in writing. He would ensure that my letter was put before the Brethren. I had not even suspected that I would need permission from the General Authorities. Glen could not predict how the Brethren would respond to such a request, but at least I had found someone who would listen and I had a chance to voice my desires. So I drafted a letter to Glen Leonard, spelling out in detail what my goals and needs were for the masks, and sent it up to Salt Lake City the next day. We could only wait and hope.

It was impossible during the following days and weeks to concentrate on my normal day-to-day work while knowing that somewhere in Salt Lake City, people who did not know of my passion and longing had the power to grant me my wish or to deny it: to launch me on a great adventure, or to shatter my dreams.

After waiting an interminable month for a reply, I was ready to withdraw my

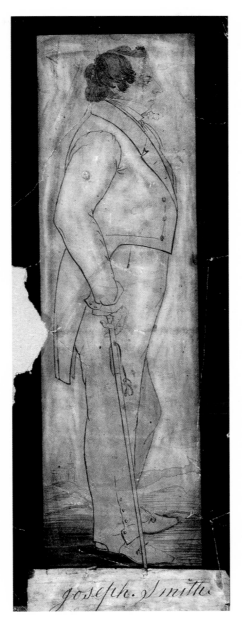

A Maudsley image of Joseph dressed in broadcloth

request. It must be impossible to get the needed permission for this project. Then I remembered a quote from Winston Churchill: "Never give up, Never give up, Never, never, never!" So I determined to try again.

About 4:00 on a Friday afternoon, I dialed Glen's number. I was going to ask him if there were any other avenue to follow to get permission to use the death masks.

Someone picked up the phone and I heard Glen's greeting. I responded, "Hi Glen, this is Shannon Tracy. Do you remember me?"

"Oh yes. How are you? I've been expecting your call. Are you ready to make arrangements to pick up the death masks?"

I was speechless. I have been accused of being able to talk the bark off an oak tree, but at that moment, my mouth did not seem to be able to work. Glen perceived at once that I did not know what he was talking about and realized that I had not received his letter. And so he told me: my proposal had been approved!

I do not know when I have experienced such euphoria. You could not have removed

A Maudsley image of Joseph

the smile from my face with sandpaper. I tried to keep my mind on Glen's directions, but there were too many plans to be made. I remember only that I made arrangements to pick up the masks the first of the next week. It was a remarkable act of self-discipline not to implore him to hold the museum open for an hour more that afternoon. The weekend was interminable.

When I met with Glen the next week, we spent some time discussing the accuracy of the known images of the Prophet. I knew that this information would be valuable later when I tried to place the correct features over the images of the death masks in my computer.

We took the elevator down to the basement. As the doors opened I saw on a steel table a small cardboard box. Glen pointed at it and I picked it up. That was it? I had them? And even though Glen continued to discuss the various images of the Prophet, I was not terribly attentive. All I could think of was the contents of this box.

The masks were shaped plaster and nothing more, but I held them like the treasures from King Tut's tomb. They were the keys to a door, to a great project. I was taking the first steps down Mulholland Drive in Nauvoo to the Mansion House. I was on my way to meet Joseph. I could feel the grass of Nauvoo under my feet and the weight of history in my hands. With modern technology and with death masks from the nineteenth century, I was going to undertake to find the Prophet in a way that had never been attempted before. Utilizing a discipline that would combine plaster casts and computer chips, I would try to re-create the living features of the man John Taylor said had done more for the salvation of the world than any other person who ever lived in it, except for Jesus Christ (see D&C 135:3).

Glen Leonard discussed with me those images of Joseph Smith that he felt were most accurate. This was vital information. Fine-tuning the features of the brothers would require all available data. The masks would give us accurate facial structures, but for the colors and textures of the skin, eyes, hair—for the detail of the external appearance—I would need to know all that could be known about these matters. But I confess that my heart and head were elsewhere that day.

As I was about to leave the museum, Glen mentioned that a lecture concerning Joseph Smith was to be given at Brigham Young University in a few days. Ronald Romig, the archivist of the Reorganized Church of Jesus Christ of Latter Day Saints (RLDS), was going to speak about a possible daguerreotype of the Prophet Joseph. Historians have speculated about the existence of a photographic image of Joseph, but nothing verifiable has ever surfaced. As a matter of fact, Glen did not give *this* daguerreotype much hope, but he thought that Ron Romig might be a source of additional useful information. The RLDS church might have access to information about the appearance of Joseph that would prove worthwhile to my study. Glen asked if I would be interested in going, and I made a note of the time and place. It seemed to me that Glen had mentioned this lecture as an afterthought, an event indirectly related to my research. Neither of us imagined the monumental implications that his simple suggestion would have in my search for Joseph.

As I left the museum, my mind was electrified with ideas and plans, and my heart was on fire with the hope of things to come.

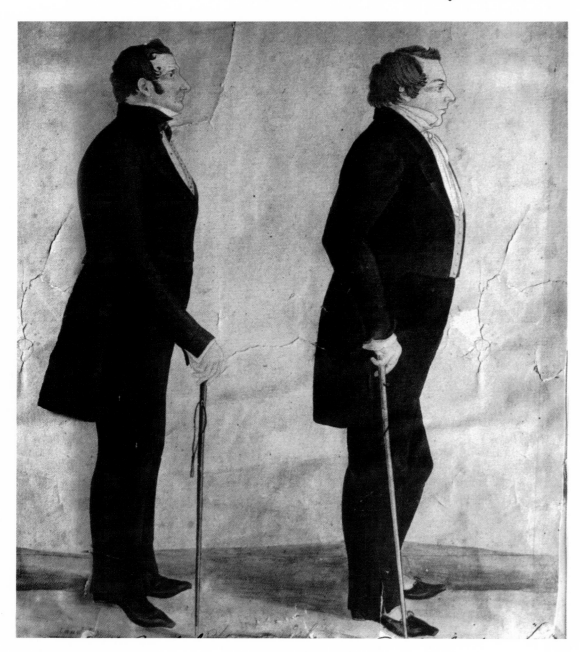

Original Maudsley portrait of Hyrum and Joseph given with a lock of Joseph's hair to Charles Lorenzo Pettit by a relative. Copies were made in 1948 from the original and given to Charles's children. This copy now in the possession of Linda Bloomquist Stratton, daughter of Edith Pettit Bloomquist.

Death Masks in 3-D

 studied the masks for hours that night. The touch and texture of them seemed almost miraculous. I had before me the final mortal images of two of the best men who had ever lived on this earth. I had been entrusted not just with the masks but with a commission to utilize them to present to the world more accurate images of Joseph and Hyrum Smith than anyone had seen since 1844.

Sitting before the masks that night, regarding them in the gentle light of a small table lamp, I had an overpowering desire to be both worthy of and equal to the challenge. This was a project for someone with both testimony and talent. I knew that others had more talent with digitizing, and I knew that others had richer testimonies. But I had both, and now I had the masks. It was time to move forward.

Late that night, after hours of studying the masks, I finally lay down to sleep. But it was a useless endeavor. Any possibilities of slumber had been driven out of my reach. I felt the weight of the responsibility. I felt honored with the opportunity. Could I bring together a team that could do this work and justify the trust and the opportunity? I had a desire to do this thing, but only if I could do it right. I did not want to add any personal artistic flair or interpretation. I did not want to show the world another version of what the Smiths might have looked like. I wanted to present the prophets so that followers could see them as their friends had seen them.

I was so caught up with the enormity of the task that I considered returning the masks to Glen. I knew my talents, but I also knew my weaknesses. Surely someone, somewhere else, had more skill than I, to do this work.

Then peace and calm settled over me. It was going to be all right.

I knew my weaknesses, but in that moment I also knew that somehow, if I desired, the task could be done. I relaxed and drifted off to sleep.

&

There are a number of ways to make a 3-D model on a computer. The simplest is to organize basic geometric forms like circles and squares in a 3-D space and then add to or take away from the shapes until the remaining figure matches the original. There are two inherent limitations with this approach. First, the final product can never be better than the artistic talent of the computer operator; and, second, the process has no algorithmic exactness to it. The final product of such an approach is substantially subjective, and my entire focus was on unconditional accuracy.

Another computer capability makes it possible to input an image by means of a laser. A highly sophisticated machine transmits and then traces a beam of light across an image. Specialized software then measures the time required for the laser light to reflect from the image back to the source. Differences in time, which are nearly infinitesimal at the speed of light, are displayed as

3-D geometry, that is, representations of height, width, and depth. This method is exceptionally accurate in applications dealing with objects whose shape and contours are regular and predictable. Its major drawback originates in the physical law that light travels only in a straight line. When the object being scanned has vacant spaces such as those behind the ears or under the eyebrows, these concealed locations are represented as solid areas.

A third option, three-dimensional digitization, was my area of expertise, and it seemed to be the best choice. To digitize an object, an operator uses a battery-powered pen with an electronic tip to trace contour lines on objects. The operator moves the pen around on the object. Each time he clicks the button, a known point is established in three-dimensional space and its location relative to all other previously identified points is specified. As the operator proceeds, a wire frame of connecting points and lines develops and creates a discernible image. In order for this method to be employed correctly the object must be graphed ahead of time with lines and intersecting points following natural valleys

and ridges. The more points and lines the operator can trace on the image map or original object, the finer the detail will be in the computed image. With sufficient lines and points, and with a trained operator, precise reproduction is possible.

I knew this was the best method to digitize the masks, but to employ it, I would need to inscribe lines and points all over them, and that, I did not have permission to do. These death masks were not the originals from 1844, but neither were they new. They appeared to have some history to them. A mold must exist somewhere. I needed copies of the masks that could be marked up.

I was not anxious to pursue this, however. The masks had been in my possession for only a short time. I felt I would appear ungrateful if I returned to Glen Leonard and said, "I need another copy of the masks, one that I can ruin." I decided to search for another way of preparing the masks for digitization without destroying their visual attractiveness. Later I learned that there is no other way.

I began to work on other requirements of the project. I needed an expert in making

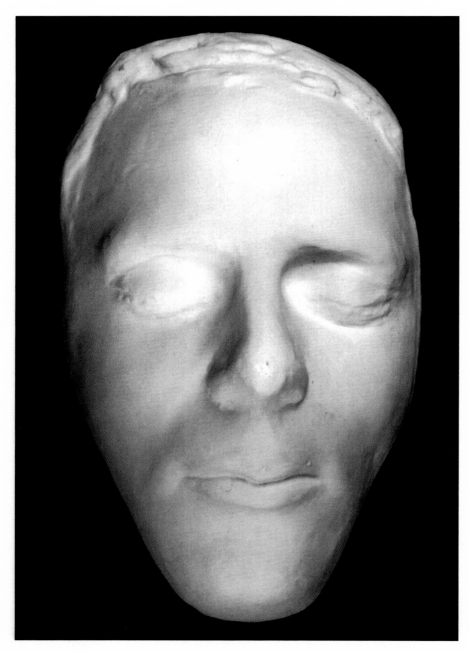

Joseph's death mask

human models in 3-D. I knew I could do the task and do it quite well, but I also knew that within a few miles of where I was sitting there lived and worked a man who was one of the foremost operators in this field.

Christopher H. Creek, managing director of Zygote Media, runs this computer company in Mapleton, Utah, along with Eric P. Merritt and Roger D. Clarke. They specialize in 3-D animation. Few who know of their work would disagree with me if I announced that they are the best in the world at what they do. Christopher Creek was the best man, and had the best team in the country, for the task in which I was now engaged. And his business was located practically in my backyard.

I had two questions: would they have the time, and could I afford them? I could see no future in just wondering, so I called Chris.

Chris is a tall, angular man with dark hair. When he is not smiling, he is about to. He loves life and he loves his work. After a few words of introduction I explained what I wanted to do and asked him if he was interested. This was like offering tuna fish to a house cat. Chris immediately offered some suggestions about the best way to approach the problem. One point Chris made absolutely clear: we would definitely need a copy of the masks that we could mark up.

We talked about a date for our first meeting, and Chris explained that he would need some time to get his equipment together, as he had recently moved to a new location. This was not a problem; I could use the interval effectively. I needed to search the written descriptions of Joseph Smith. I wanted to gather a great number of descriptions and then search them for consensus about the features of the Prophet Joseph.

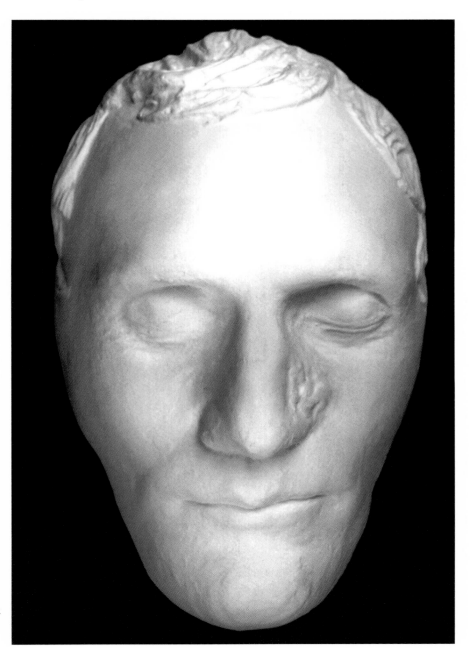

Hyrum's death mask

CHAPTER 4

Joseph, the Man

oseph Smith was a man of great charisma, and his physical presence seemed always to make an impact on those about him. But those who characterized him never seemed to be able to quit with a simple physical description. The admiration they felt always compelled them to speak of his character. Again and again as I read those words of love and respect, I paused in wonder. Joseph was indeed a man whose influence reached deeper than the surfaces of people. His work was done in the heart.

Wandle Mace recalled a time when she heard the Prophet speak from the stairs at the back of a house. She wrote, "This is the first time I ever heard the prophet speak, and I shall never forget his words. . . . He had a free and easy manner, not the least affectation yet bold and independent and very interesting and eloquent in speech."[2] Parley P. Pratt, a genius with a pen, gave a description of startling clarity, but then went on to say, "His countenance was ever mild, affable, beaming with intelligence and benevolence; mingled with a look of interest and an unconscious smile, or cheerfulness, and entirely free from all restraint or affectation of gravity."[3]

Matthew S. Davis, a member of Congress, reported, "He is not an educated man. Everything he says is said in a manner to leave an impression that is sincere. There is no levity, no fanaticism, no want of dignity in his deportment."[4] Lydia Bailey Knight echoed similar themes: "[Joseph has] a striking countenance, and with manners at once majestic yet gentle, dignified yet exceedingly pleasant."[5] James Palmer thought that Joseph presented a "formidable appearance" but noted also that Joseph was "a man of gentlemanly bearing."[6] Josiah Quincy's impression of the Prophet has often been

A Maudsley image of Joseph Smith

quoted. He found Joseph to be "a hearty, athletic fellow," who had a "commanding appearance."[7]

Edward Stevenson depicted Joseph as "a plain but noble-looking man."[8] Gilbert Belnap wrote: "I was introduced to the Prophet, whose mild and penetrating glance denoted great depth of tough and extensive forethought. While standing before his penetrating gaze, he seemed to read the very recesses of my heart."[9]

Selected excerpts follow from a number of written descriptions of the Prophet Joseph Smith. Although I experienced substantial difficulty in confining my notes to his physical attributes, I discovered a wealth of information, and examples of what I learned follow. I have considered his features separately in order to allow the reader an opportunity to visualize each characteristic in its place.

HEIGHT

"he stood over six feet tall."[10]
"He was about six feet tall."[11]
" six feet high . . ."[12]
"measuring over six feet in height . . ."[13]
"tall and slender—thin favored."[14]

WEIGHT

"In his mature years he weighed about two hundred pounds."[15]
"Brother Joseph was a man weighing about two hundred pounds."[16]
"My father . . . weighed two hundred and ten pounds."[17]
"This 'prophet' is a man of large frame—tending to corpulency."[18]

HAIR

"light hair and very little beard . . ."[19]
"His hair [was] a golden brown."[20]
"His head [was] crowned with a mass of soft, wavy hair."[21]
"His hair is quite light and fine."[22]
"His hair was of a flaxen color."[23]
"His hair had turned from tow-colored to light auburn."[24]
"light chestnut hair . . ."[25]

EYES and EYEBROWS

"handsome blue eyes . . ."[26]
On the color of his eyes there is almost universal agreement. Parley P. Pratt,

Wandle Mace, George Q. Cannon, George Moore, and many others all specify the color blue. But there are other interesting observations as well: "But the Prophet's most remarkable feature is his eye; not that it is very large, or very bright—very thoughtful or very restless—even very deep in its expression or location; for it is usually neither of these. The hue is light hazel, and is shaded, and at times, almost veiled, by the longest, thickest light lashes you ever saw belonging to a man, whatever the facts respecting the 'dear ladies.' The brows are, also, light and thick—indeed, precisely of that description called beetle-brow."[27]

"intelligent eyes . . ."[28]

" . . . eyes standing prominently out upon his light complexion."[29]

"large eyes of bluish gray . . ."[30]

"blue eyes set far back in the head . . ."[31]

"His eyes were shaded by long light eye lashes and bushy eyebrows that were not arched, but ran straight across. The whole arrangement of his eyes, lashes, and brows is said to have produced an unusual or even magnetic effect."[32]

FOREHEAD

"His forehead is white, without a furrow."[33]

"a retreating forehead . . ."[34]

NOSE

"His nose was long and straight."[35]

"a long nose . . ."[36]

"a prominent nose . . ."[37]

"a Roman nose . . ."[38]

LIPS, MOUTH, CHIN

"lips thin rather than thick . . ."[39]

"his mouth was narrow, and his upper lip rather long and a little inclined to be thick."[40]

"His mouth was about as wide as his chin disclosing a pleasing expression or perhaps unconscious smile."[41]

"upper lip full and rather protruding . . ."[42]

"His chin was a little tipped . . ."[43]

"chin broad and square . . ."[44]

"I heard the real and perfect voice of the Prophet, even to the whistle, as in years past caused by the loss of a tooth said to have been broken out by the mob at Hyrum."[45]

COMPLEXION

"of a light complexion . . ."[46]

"his complexion was one of transparency so rare as to be remarkable."[47]

"fair complexion . . ."[48]

"His complexion was of corpselike paleness and waxy."[49]

"His complexion was fair."[50]

SHOULDERS and CHEST

"His chest and shoulders are broad and muscular."[51]

"Though his chest was broad and full, his shoulders were perhaps inclined a bit toward being round."[52]

"He had a large full chest."[53]

LEGS and FEET

"fine legs . . ."[54]

"His hands were small, but his feet were large on long legs."[55]

"He was about six feet high, what might be termed long legged, with big feet."[56]

Early engraving of Joseph Smith

An Unexpected Discovery

The symposium on the daguerreotype thought to be of Joseph Smith was sponsored by F.A.R.M.S. (Foundation for Ancient Research and Mormon Studies) at BYU. Ron Romig said that the daguerreotype had been given to the RLDS church in 1968 by a family that believed they were distant relatives of Joseph Smith. They claimed to have a family Bible, a journal, and other Smith family personal items. Family tradition indicated the image was of Joseph Smith, taken shortly before his death.

No hard evidence exists for such an image, but historical circumstances made its existence possible. Two daguerrotypists were at work in Nauvoo in early 1844. One of them, Lucian Rose Foster, rented a room from Joseph Smith at the Mansion House. A few early Church brethren report sitting for daguerreotypes by Foster. It seems reasonable Foster sought permission to make an image of the Prophet Joseph and the Patriarch Hyrum simply for advertising purposes.[57]

The image had suffered from the passage of time and was not of high quality. Some of its characteristics did not seem to belong to the Joseph whose images I had studied. One feature captured my attention immediately, however. The left eyebrow and cheekbone of the man in the daguerreotype were slightly lower than the right eyebrow and cheekbone. This facial characteristic is a distinctive feature of Joseph's death mask. I wanted to have a closer look at this likeness, to scan it into my computer so that I could enlarge and clean it, then enhance it by manipulating the contrasts and tones. I wondered what this image would look like as an overlay to Joseph's death mask.

After the presentation, I remained in the conference room, hoping to discuss the daguerreotype with Mr. Romig and to let him know

a little of what I was trying to accomplish. When the rest of the crowd had departed, I introduced myself and explained what I was about to do with the death masks. Ron perceived immediately the symbiotic nature of our studies, realizing what I was doing could be of help to him in proving or disproving the authenticity of the daguerreotype.

I explained to Ron the difficulty of completing the rest of the head of the Prophet, since I was required to work primarily with death masks, which revealed only the front of the face.

Ron informed me then of a most significant event—in 1928 the bodies of the brothers had been disinterred and moved to their current resting place, and at that time several photographs had been taken of the skulls. Ron had hoped to find a way to show the correlation of the skulls, death masks, and the daguerreotype.

Skull photos! I had never imagined that such data might exist. I told Ron that with the pictures of the skulls I could make the 3-D images more accurate. I then briefly explained the process by which those images could be positioned in the size and pose of the daguerreotype so that we could see clearly how well they matched. I suggested that if I had access to the photographs of the skulls, both his work and mine might greatly benefit. I asked if it would be possible to obtain permission to use the photos for research. Ron explained to me that the RLDS church had never released the images. However, he indicated that if I would write a letter describing my research and how the photos could further the project, he would see that my request was put in front of the right people. Ron and I realized that we could work together on this matter—that what I was attempting to do might eventually be of great benefit to him. I told Ron that I would need to finish my work on the models before I began to compare my research with the daguerreotype so that it would not influence the work on the 3-D models.

Ron and I exchanged addresses and a promise to trade information. I left the room with a new obsession. I knew that with access to the photos of the skulls of Joseph and Hyrum, we could make an incredibly accurate reproduction of the brothers, for we would have both the skulls and the surface images of the faces captured by the death masks. We would not have to search for skulls that we hoped were similar. Forensic artists often make renderings of people, working from just their skulls, but we had actual images of the flesh (the death masks) as well to work from. I knew that another sleepless night of planning would follow, but I did not care. I went home and penned the letter Ron had requested and had it ready for the next day.

With increased enthusiasm and no viable alternative, I called Glen Leonard again and explained my need for a set of death masks that could be inscribed with the grid pattern required by 3-D imaging. I made a sincere effort to inform him of the importance of these new masks to this project. To my relief, Glen felt that there should be no problem. He promised to make contact with the gentleman who had made other sets for the museum to determine the time required and the cost involved. Glen told me that I would have to cover the cost of the new casting. I gladly accepted the offer and thanked him for the help.

The masks, which cost $65.00, were ready just after the beginning of the year. All my fears had been groundless.

CHAPTER 6

"To Seal the Testimony": Death Comes to Carthage

he study of the written descriptions had deepened my knowledge of the Prophet. People who knew Joseph only in passing, people who came to ridicule or to expose, had few complimentary things to say. But those who knew him well almost invariably loved him. I, too, was learning to know and love him better. From that love had grown this great desire to re-create his true image.

The time over the holidays I spent in research while I waited for a new set of masks to be prepared and for permission to have access to the photos of the skeletal remains of the brothers. I was also waiting for Chris Creek to bring his new business on line.

I learned that some have questioned the accuracy of the death masks. The trauma of the Martyrdom might have caused the flesh to swell, and loss of muscle tension might have caused the jaws to drop. But reported customs of the 1840s included closing the eyes, tying up the chin, and occasionally cooling the body with ice. Dr. Willard Richards would certainly have done what he could in the night he spent with the bodies following the attack on the jail.[58] We know that he spent the night in preparing the bodies for burial.

Therefore, even though the masks were made the day following the death of these men, decent evidence exists for supposing that the images are accurate. I have spent many hours studying the masks, and I have concluded that they do reflect evidence of trauma at the time of death or shortly thereafter. However, many of the measurements and features of their faces, and their over-all appearances, would have remained constant.

Some might question the historicity of the masks. However, abundant evidence indicates that contemporaries of the brothers accepted

A Maudsley painting of Joseph in his Nauvoo Legion general's uniform

the masks as genuine. And with the power of the computer and the photographs of the skulls, we would be able to examine the masks and verify their accuracy in previously impossible ways.

I turned my attention to the actual events of the Martyrdom. I needed to know exactly what had happened to the Smiths at the time of their deaths and immediately following.

It was a warm and humid Thursday afternoon in Carthage, Illinois. June that year had been rainy, and the county roads were nearly impassable. A brief shower had dampened that June afternoon, but by 4:30 or 5:00, the precipitation had stopped. Joseph and Hyrum had been in jail since Tuesday afternoon, the twenty-fifth. They had come to the county seat to answer charges of riot, charges that had arisen from the destruction of the press of the *Nauvoo Expositor*.

But after a preliminary hearing at which bail was posted and the case bound over for the next hearing of the circuit court, the Church leaders had been forced into jail without any kind of hearing on the charge of *treason!* The Smiths were

surprised by this new charge. They did not know that mob leaders had collected eighteen charges to be used against the Mormon leaders, one after another, until one was successful.[59]

A company of the Carthage Grays (the local militia) marched Joseph and Hyrum

Joseph giving his farewell address to the Saints in Nauvoo prior to his incarceration in Carthage Jail

and their companions to their place of confinement. These were the same soldiers that on the twenty-fifth had three times publicly threatened Joseph and Hyrum with death. These were the same brave warriors who would be guarding the jail with un-loaded weapons when the mob attacked. No doubt they were also the first to flee Carthage when false warning of a Mormon counterattack swept through town.

The morning of the twenty-seventh had passed slowly. Joseph was distraught. He had frequently prophesied his own death, but the impending reality of the event, intensified by threats of the guards below, the departure from Carthage of the governor, his longing for his family, and his desire to speak once more to the Saints in Nauvoo, had discouraged him.

Each of his companions—John Taylor, Willard Richards, and his brother Hyrum— had tried to encourage him, but without

success. Hyrum went so far as to read three accounts contained in the Book of Mormon of God freeing his servants from prison by his own power.[60] But the stories of Nephi

Engraving of Carthage Jail in 1855

and Lehi, Alma and Amulek, and the Three Nephites did not enliven Joseph. He was certain that in his case there would be no such divine intervention. Trying to relieve the undiluted gloom, Joseph asked a

reluctant John Taylor to sing in his rich tenor voice. Elder Taylor selected a song that had recently become popular in Nauvoo, "A Poor Wayfaring Man of Grief." The text, based on Matthew 25, was a fitting overture for the drama to follow.

Members of the Warsaw Militia attacked the jail about 5:00 p.m. on the afternoon of June 27. Joseph and Hyrum were confined in the jailor's bedroom on the second floor at the right side of the landing. The militiamen came from the woods northeast of the jail. One (or more) made his way to the door of the bedroom and tried to force the door, which was being held from the other side by Joseph, Hyrum, John Taylor, and Willard Richards. Evidently thinking the door locked, a mobster fired a ball through the keyhole. This shot harmed no one, but its passage indicated that the door, con-structed of half-inch common panel, was no protection.

Three of those within, all except Hyrum, moved toward the front or south part of the room. Willard Richards indicates that Hyrum backed up two-thirds of the way across the room when a ball, fired through the door, struck him at the base of the nose on the left side. The angle of the bullet hole in the door, which still stands at the entrance to the jailor's bedroom, suggests, however, that Hyrum could not have been so far from the door when the fatal ball struck him. Any distance of more than three feet would probably have caused the ball to pass harmlessly over his head. Willard Richards reported that before Hyrum fell, a shot fired from outside the east window entered his back. The ball passed through his body with sufficient force to pulverize the watch in his front vest pocket, but it did not break the skin in front. As Hyrum lay on the floor, another ball from the doorway grazed his leg and his right chest and entered his head under his chin near the throat. Another ball entered his left leg at the knee or just grazed it, and another penetrated his right leg in the side of the thigh. Evidence for these other wounds received by Hyrum is found in his clothing, which is currently in the possession of Eldred G. Smith, Patriarch Emeritus to The Church of Jesus Christ of Latter-day Saints. None of the skull photos shows exit wounds in the head area.

Following the death of his brother, Joseph discharged into the stairwell a small six-shot pepper-box pistol given to him by Cyrus Wheelock. The gun fired three times and misfired three times. Three men were wounded.[61]

Joseph recognized that there was no safety in the room. He knew that he and Hyrum were the objects of the attack. He certainly hoped that the act he now attempted might save the lives of friends who were still within the bedroom. He stepped calmly from the corner where Willard Richards had attempted to shield the Prophet with his own body, dropped his

Frederick Piercy engraving (1855) of a woman pointing out the bullet holes in the wall at Carthage Jail

pistol on the floor near his brother's corpse, and sprang to the open window. Before he could throw himself out he was shot two to three times. Willard Richards recorded that Joseph received two balls in the back from the doorway, and one in the chest from outside the window.[62] He then fell out the window and to the ground below, landing on his left side.

I am moved deeply by this final mortal act of Joseph Smith. That he should die, as he had lived, giving service, is profoundly important. At least in part because of his heroic act, the other two men in the room, John Taylor and Willard Richards, survived to bear witness of the events of the Martyrdom and to provide important church service.

Eyewitness accounts differ on whether or not Joseph was dead when he hit the ground, but evidence suggests that he was shot and abused afterward. At least two accounts mention that the Prophet was struck in the face after his fall from the window. In a letter written in October of 1844, one claiming to have been a member of the mob tells us that Joseph "appeared stunned by the fall. I struck him in the

face and said, 'Old Jo, damn you, where are you now.'"[63]

Henry M. Harmon, of Carthage, was at the jail during the attack. In an affidavit given in the LDS Church Historian's Office in Salt Lake City on April 14, 1857, he declared: "Joseph . . . leaped from the window, when the mob fired upon him and he fell dead. The fifer of the Warsaw Company came running into the jail yard as Joseph fell dead, and brandishing his fife over Joseph . . . struck him several times in the head with his pewter fife."[64] Other accounts contend that Joseph was still alive when he came out of the window. Thomas Dixon, who was near the jail, reported seeing blood on Joseph's clothing, but affirmed

that "he was not dead when he fell—he raised himself up against the well curb."[65] Governor Ford's aide-de-camp, Edward A. Bedell, in an 1854 interview in Salt Lake City, stated that Joseph lived "some time" after he fell from the window.[66] The following quote is in the *Historical Record*.

"Among the murderers outside [of Carthage Jail] was a man, barefoot and bareheaded, without a coat, his shirtsleeves

Frederick Piercy 1855 engraving of the well and summer kitchen at Carthage Jail

Early artist's conception of the Nauvoo Temple

rolled up above his elbows and his pants above his knees; he lifted Joseph and propped him against the south side of the well curb, which stood a few feet from the jail. Col. Levi Williams then ordered four men to shoot him. They stood about eight feet from the curb and fired simultaneously. A slight cringe of the body was noticed as the balls struck him, and he fell on his face."[67]

It seems we must wait for a millennial interview to ascertain the correctness of the varying accounts. But taken together they give strong evidence of the trauma inflicted on Joseph at the time of his death.

About 3:00 p.m. the next day, Willard Richards arrived in Nauvoo with the bodies of Joseph and Hyrum. At the Mansion House, preparation began immediately for the viewing and the burial of the Prophet and the Patriarch. George Cannon made death masks. Dimick B. Huntington, assisted by William Marks and William D. Huntington, cleansed the bodies thoroughly and reported the following:

"Joseph was shot in the right breast, also under the heart, in the lower part of his bowels and the right side, and on the back part of his right hip. One ball had come out at the right shoulder-blade."[68]

Later, the Huntingtons reported the same wounds, but they mentioned one

more wound at the right collarbone. This firsthand report of the wounds received by Joseph is invaluable but somewhat lacking in precision. The testimony of those who made the examination certifies that Joseph received no wounds in the head, as had Hyrum, but only in the body.

For the viewing by family and Church members on June 29, the bodies were placed in coffins covered with black velvet and lined with white cambric. These coffins were placed in rough-hewn pine boxes. When the viewing was completed, the coffins were removed from the boxes and concealed in the Mansion House. The pine boxes were weighted with bags of sand and nailed shut, placed in a hearse, driven to the graveyard, and there interred with traditional decorum. This was done to prevent the stealing or mutilation of the bodies by enemies of the Smiths and the Church. Reports received in Nauvoo indicated that enemies of the Prophet had offered a reward of $1,000 for the head of Joseph Smith. That night the graves were disturbed by those seeking the reward.[69]

About midnight, a company of trusted friends, one carrying a musket, removed the bodies and coffins from the Mansion House and carried them to the unfinished and roofless Nauvoo House, where they were buried in the basement. A timely summer thunderstorm obliterated all traces of the burial.[70]

Traditions vary regarding the details of the final burial of the martyred brothers. But some facts are clear enough to provide a reasonable framework for the event. It is apparent that the reburial of the bodies, during the late fall or early winter of 1844–1845, was conducted with much secrecy in the darkness of night. The two

Smiths, under the direction of Emma, were moved to the family cemetery southwest of the Homestead and buried under a little out-building, referred to at times as the bee-house. Safely hidden there, they could keep company with other deceased members of the family, while living family members provided protection for the site.

The deceased children of the Prophet Joseph were later moved and buried at the same site. At that time, excavators learned that two of Hyrum's teeth were loose inside his mouth, presumed to be a result of the ball that struck his face and took his life. The disfigurement of his jaw was not noted when he was laid out for viewing and burial since his jaws were tied up in accordance with the custom of the day.

Frederick Piercy 1855 engraving of the ruins of the Nauvoo Temple

CHAPTER 7

The Search for the Unknown Grave

 third of a century passed while the brothers lay in their graves in a place fewer and fewer people could point to with certainty. Emma died on April 30, 1879. The little out-building had by that time long since ceased to exist, but Emma thought she remembered its location. According to an unverified source, Emma requested burial exactly 23 paces from the southeast corner of the Homestead.[71] If this report is accurate, her request was either misunderstood or disregarded, for her grave was uncovered at that distance from the southwest corner. Even *her* burial location was uncertain. A monument constructed sometime later was placed three feet from her actual burial site.

Difficulties increased when the Smiths no longer occupied the property. Vegetation withered and weeds abounded. Pigs wandered the grave area freely. Concerned by reports about the neglect of what should have been a sacred spot, the general conference of the RLDS church assigned the construction of a suitable monument, and visits were made and plans discussed but nothing of a permanent nature was done.

Joseph Smith III visited the Homestead in 1908 and, according to the account of one who was there, pointed out the precise location of the bodies of Joseph and Hyrum.[72] That event was apparently also forgotten, or at least neglected, in the subsequent search for the bodies. And there were few others who could give accurate assistance. In 1883, Joseph Smith III indicated that probably no more than half a dozen living persons knew the location of the graves.[73]

The brothers rested untroubled on the sloping ground between the Homestead and the Mississippi until about 1910 when a series of dams along the river began to cause dramatic alteration in the level

Emma's grave marker; to the left, not seen, is her second husband's grave.

The Presiding Bishop of the RLDS church wrote to W. O. Hands, a civil engineer well respected by leaders of the church. Hands had worked in the construction of electric railways in the East and had done additional work on dams, roads, and railways. He had a personal interest in the construction of the Keokuk Dam and had been preoccupied for some time in searching the records for the actual location of the graves of Joseph and Hyrum. Hands was asked to visit the church property in Nauvoo and to make an assessment of

water damage and of the liability of the Keokuk and Hamilton Water and Power Company.

Hands was convinced that the encroachment of the water onto the Homestead property was a violation of an agreement between the church and the power company, an agreement that gave the power company rights to increase water levels only to specific contour lines. Hands certified that the levels of the river had passed those lines. However, power company officials were unwilling to act on the

and flow of the water. The construction of a dam at Keokuk, south of Nauvoo, turned the sometimes impassible rapids just below Nauvoo into Lake Cooper. The creation of this lake became a grave concern for the leadership of the RLDS church, for it seemed evident to them that the rising water would sooner or later become a danger to the property below the Homestead and perhaps even to the graves of the Smiths. The Homestead had been given to the church by Frederick M. Smith in 1908, and the southern exposure of that property was suffering substantial erosion due to the rising waters.

A stereoscopic photo of the Old Homestead about 1904 with Emma's grave marker in foreground

matter. They denied culpability at first and then, in 1920, tried to contain the problem by placing a restraining wall of rock along the edge of the property next to the river. But reports issued in August of that year indicated that the stone wall was inadequate and that erosion continued.

Seven more years passed. Lake Cooper continued to deepen behind the dam at Keokuk. The RLDS church continued to claim that the power company was liable for the loss of church assets. Numerous letters were sent, but the company, in laying the rock along the edge of the river, had taken

the last action it would take in this matter for many years.

On December 30, 1927, a meeting was held in the office of the president of the RLDS church. Hands and others attended, and Hands took notes at the meeting. President Fred M. Smith believed the bodies to be under a "spring house" or "ice house" that stood near the river, where it was currently in some danger from the rising water. President Smith also said that Hyrum's skull could be identified by the shot *through the right side of the nose below the right eye*.[74]

This description of a wound to Hyrum's head would have great significance later when the bodies were found and when they were reburied. The RLDS church was not in possession of the death masks, nor were they familiar with the eyewitness accounts by Willard Richards and those who prepared the bodies for burial. All of this firsthand information indicates that the fatal shot to Hyrum's head was on the *left side of the nose, and below the left eye*.

On January 4, 1928, William O. Hands was given a charge to locate the bodies, to put an end to disagreements about their final resting place, and to "build a concrete

Old Homestead as seen from the Mississippi River. Note bric-a-brac the power company placed at the waterline to help prevent erosion.

W. O. Hands

Mississippi might cause flooding that could wash away the entire area.

Hands arrived in Nauvoo on Tuesday, January 9, 1928, with forty dollars to pay his help and with a desire to do the work as quietly as possible. No buildings were evident from the southern side of the Homestead to the water's edge. He had no idea where the "spring house" spoken of by President Smith was located, so he examined old photos belonging to a Nauvoo citizen until he located the site of the old brick building described by the RLDS church president. It appeared to be near the shore of Cooper Lake.

The actual digging began on January 10. The laborers located the foundation of an old building, thought to be the "spring house" (also referred to as the "ice house" and the "old barn") and dug deeply and thoroughly in that area. The excavation, which descended three feet below the level of the nearby river, continually filled with

box to hold [the] bodies that will serve as a base for the shaft."[75] One other, most significant reason has been given for the decision to locate and rebury the bodies of the Martyrs: concern over the rising water. Fred M. Smith's statement was that the bodies were under the "spring house" near the water's edge. The spring thaw combined with the increasing water levels of the

Workers digging below the foundation of the spring house, which is near the river. Note they are working below water level and need constantly to bail out the water.

Emma's grave marker with intense trenching around it. The bushes at the foot of the marker are lilacs, which Emma adored. Emma was actually found on this side of the bushes three feet below her marker— not directly under it. The trench at the left of the photo is where the brothers were found in the foundation of the bee house.

water which needed to be bailed, a punishing task in the January weather. Other trenches were dug to the east and the west, for 17 and 42 feet respectively.[76] But by Thursday, the twelfth, even though the area of the "spring house" was thoroughly excavated, no human remains had been located.

On Friday, workers turned uphill and began to trench around the marker of Emma's grave, thinking that Emma had perhaps been buried near her husband and her brother-in-law. Sometime before noon, the men located a coffin and a skeleton three feet east of the northeast corner of

Emma's grave marker. Hopes soared and then plummeted when the remains were determined to belong to a woman. A woman's hair comb and remnants of the brown silk robe in which Emma had been buried made identification positive by those who remembered her burial.[77] Excavations of three feet under Emma's marker showed no evidence of any grave ever having been there.

Workers also dug a hole seven feet deep just north of Emma's marker. But by Saturday, when Mr. Hands wrote his second letter to church headquarters in Independence, the workers had still not uncovered any evidence of the graves or remains of the Prophet and the Patriarch. They were at a loss to know where to dig next. Hands asked for more direction and suggested that the Brethren pray and, if appropriate, fast for the success of his efforts. RLDS members in Nauvoo evidently planned on doing the same. Sunday meetings continued late in the evening and focused on that one issue. But the day came to a close with no discernible promptings.

Early the next morning, William Hands returned to the yard of the Homestead and surveyed the mounds of earth and the

The first evidence of the foundation of the bee house is visible here, as the workers begin to expose it.

trenches resulting from most of a week of work. Hands, with what he believed to be an inspired gesture, swept his light across a section of unexcavated ground and whispered to himself, "We will explore this place today."[78]

At 8:00 on January 16, the work commenced anew. By 10:00 the workmen had located the four sides of the foundation of a small out-building about eight feet square. Earlier trenches were within inches of this structure, but it had remained undiscovered. After announcing this find, Hands wrote, "About four feet below the surface we came upon a brick floor. This was removed, and working very carefully, we now came upon and uncovered a skull easily recognized as that of Hyrum by the bullet hole under the eye."[79] In a letter written the next day to the Presidency and the Bishopric, Hands stated, "At 2:10 we uncovered the head of Hyrum, easily recognized by the bullet hole just below the right eye."[80] Hands based these statements on the information given him by President Fred M. Smith the previous December. No one who viewed the remains seems to have doubted the accuracy of the identification, although, as I will attempt to prove, the assumption on which it was based was in error.

The rest of this skeleton was uncovered, and then the remains identified as those of Joseph were found a little south of the first body. The second skull was in much worse condition. Only the top of the skull remained intact. The lower facial bones were nearly all gone. Hands attributed the preservation of the first skull to a large flat rock that rested exactly over the skull and protected it.

Word was immediately sent to the proper officials, and on Thursday, the nineteenth of January, President Smith and others arrived in Nauvoo. With their permission, the skulls were removed to the

© RLDS church

This photograph shows the skulls in the gravesite as they were unearthed. Far right is the RLDS Hyrum framed in by two sheets of newspaper, and top center, the RLDS Joseph, just below another newspaper sheet. The papers and a sheet were placed over the skulls to help prevent casual onlookers from seeing the remains.

Mansion House, where photographs and measurements were taken. These photos of the skeletal remains of the Martyrs are located in the Archives of the RLDS church. They have, until the present time, been unavailable to the public. These were the photos that Ron Romig had mentioned to me, the photos that could prove invaluable to my research with the masks.

Several measurements were taken of the skulls while they were in the Mansion House. One of the photos shows a ruler and offers some size comparison and, perhaps, evidence of the tool used for the measurements. However, the measurements as recorded offer no precise locations on the skulls to indicate the zones and lines of measurement—the starting and stopping points of each measurement.

That deficiency, together with the extreme difficulty of making accurate calculations of the curves of these skulls with an inflexible wooden instrument, renders the numbers nearly useless except for overall size comparison.

Now that the bodies of Joseph and Hyrum had been located, Hands was concerned that a proper resting place be provided for them. He recommended in his January 17 letter that the church pay to construct a three-foot thick slab of concrete in a ten-foot square. Joseph and Hyrum should be interred in the center of the slab in boxes a foot wide and deep and six feet long. He was also anxious that

the body of Emma be moved to lie beside her first husband. Hands himself placed the

© 1993 RLDS church

Above: RLDS Hyrum skull on the left, RLDS Joseph skull on the right. In the foreground, Joseph's pocket watch is lying atop a wooden ruler. This ruler may have been the tool used to make the skull measurements.

bones of the three bodies in silk-lined boxes.

Four members of the LDS church were at the reburial. Samuel O. Bennion, president of the Central States Mission, had read

in the paper about the search for the bodies. When he learned that Fred M. Smith had gone to Nauvoo, he called on the phone and received permission to see the skeletal remains and the reburial, provided he was in Nauvoo no later than 2:00 p.m. the following day when the remains would be reinterred. He and three companions drove all night and arrived in Nauvoo the next day in time to watch the photographing and measuring of the skulls in an upper room of the Mansion House.

Although President Bennion was pleased to be in Nauvoo as a witness for

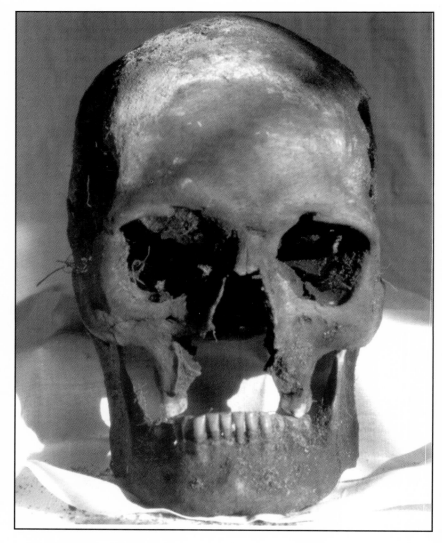

RLDS Hyrum skull, side profile and front view. Note the sharp break of the bone of the upper jaw area compared to the worn zygomatic area on the side. Also note that the jaw is out of position, protruding too far forward because the bottom of the jaw is lying flat on the table.

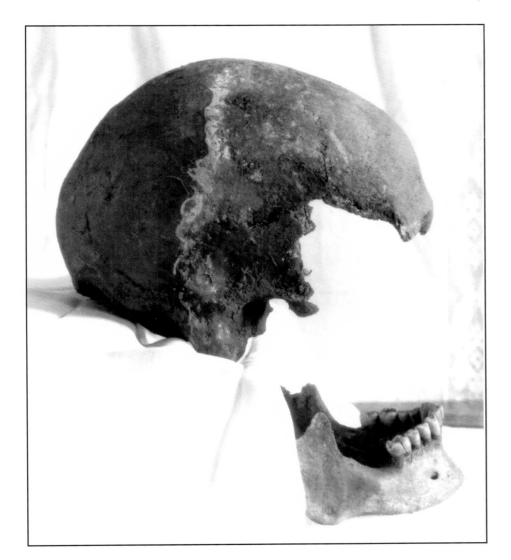

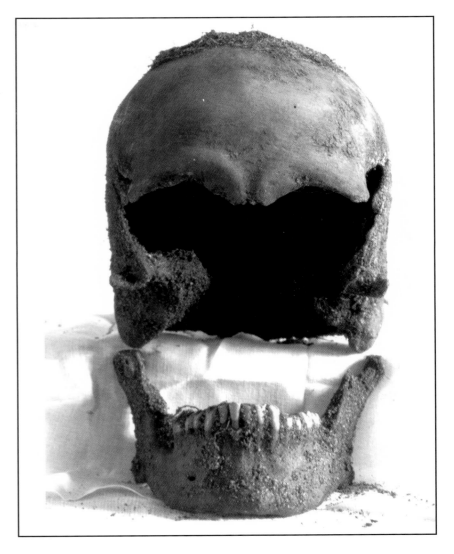

RLDS Joseph, side profile and front view. Notice the large amount of trauma to the front and base of the skull. Also, note that the back of the jaw is intact, hidden under the folds of the drapery in the left photograph. Note also the missing molar and the large amount of wear to the lower teeth.

Left: Workers digging the new gravesite next to the fence, close to the Homestead. Notice in the background the tarp tent that covers the site of the brothers' remains.

Right: The new gravesite as it appears after the foundation of concrete has been poured and the boxes that house the remains are in place. Sand has been added around the boxes. The remains are from left to right: Emma, RLDS Joseph, RLDS Hyrum. The boxes are lined with white cloth and the remains were placed therein by W. O. Hands as close to the natural positon as possible. Planks will be nailed to the tops and concrete poured over them to seal the graves.

Left: Emma's grave marker and the bushes to its right. Just past the American flag is the grave location of the brothers, which has a tarp tent over the top to protect it from the elements. The flag is in the hole itself. To the left of Emma's marker is a dark spot that marks the location of the new gravesite being prepared.

Above: New gravesite. Note that W. O. Hands has moved the flag to the new burial location.

Left: New gravesite just after final clean-up was completed. Note the Nauvoo House in the right of the photo and the Homestead on the left.

New grave markers for Emma, Joseph, and Hyrum were made from the stone marking Emma's original site. The stone was turned over, cut into three parts, and engraved with the names, birth and death years, and reinternment date.

the Utah church, he was saddened by the events taking place. In a letter written the next day to LDS President Heber J. Grant, he said, "I could hardly keep the tears back when I saw these men handling these skulls like they were just common, ordinary skulls, and I said to Fred M., 'Why didn't you let the bodies of these men rest where they were?'"[81]

RLDS President Smith explained his desire to know the true location of the graves and also alluded to a rumor that Brigham Young had taken the bodies to Salt Lake City and placed them in the Salt Lake Temple.[82] No mention was made of the early concerns caused by the rising water, a concern now seen to be unnecessary as the remains were found so high on the property that they were never in danger.

A considerable amount of publicity about the exhumation and reinterment of Joseph and Hyrum Smith focused on the animosity generated by this act. Joseph Fielding Smith, Jr., the grandson of Hyrum, made no apology for his accusations. He felt that the bodies should never have been moved and that doing so was an "unholy and sacrilegious act."[83] At the very least, Utah Mormons felt that it was improper for the RLDS church to proceed in such an action without notification of the descendants of Hyrum in Utah.

President Fred M. Smith replied that his only desire was to adequately mark the graves and to provide a monument at some future time.[84]

In spite of the disputation from the two sides of the family as to the real purpose for the locating of the bodies and their reburial, there is one matter over which there was no disagreement. Those who witnessed all or part of the unearthing, photographing, and reburial of these remains concur that they were the remains of Joseph and Hyrum. No one has ever raised a question about this. And I knew that if we used the images of the death masks overlaid on computer images of the skull photos and found that they matched, it should be possible to provide nearly indisputable proof of their identity.

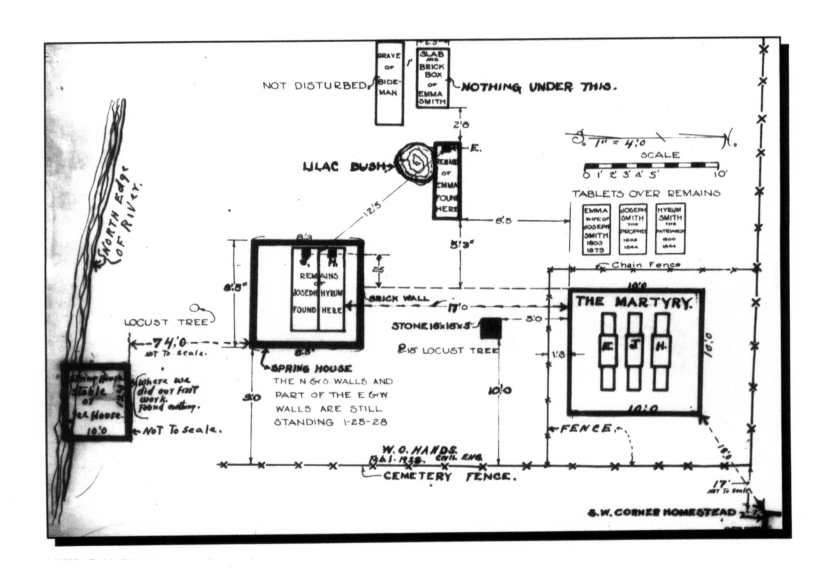

Map made by W. O. Hands of the excavation site in January 1928

Forensic Evidence: A Closer Look

ven though feelings about the locating and reburying of the bodies were ardent and at times bitter in 1928, from my more modern perspective, the photos taken could be of great benefit. They would provide a solid, verifiable foundation against which to test the 3-D images of the death masks that I was creating. They would move me much closer to the actual images of the Prophet and his brother.

I was delighted at the timely response of the RLDS church to my request. Within weeks I received copies of the photos and the permission to both use and publish them. These photos had never been outside of the archives of the RLDS church since they were placed there following the events in Nauvoo. A few had been allowed to view them and an artist had been allowed to trace the outline of the photographic images, but no one had been given permission to publish the photos nor even to remove copies of them from the church archives. They are presented in this volume with deepest gratitude to the RLDS church for their permission.

I spent some time examining the photos and determined to begin my study of the skulls with the photographs of the one that was most intact, which I will refer to as the RLDS Hyrum. This skull would clearly provide the most information in my efforts to match it with the proper death mask. I knew that the death masks were correct, and I felt that I needed to demonstrate with high probability that the photographs were indeed of the skulls of Joseph and Hyrum, rather than some other people buried at the Homestead. This I could confirm by overlaying the images of the masks on the images of the skull photos in the computer.

I had access now to important evidence relating to the physical

appearance of the Joseph and Hyrum Smith, but I knew that I needed the assistance of an expert, someone who knew a great deal more than I did about anatomy. I spoke with acquaintances in the field of medicine and also with individuals involved in the forensic sciences. One name was mentioned more than any other: Dr. Kent Van De Graaff, formerly a professor of anatomy at Brigham Young University. Chris Creek was acquainted with Dr. Van De Graaff and had done some work for him in the past. I called Dr. Van De Graaff, explained what I was trying to do, and asked if he

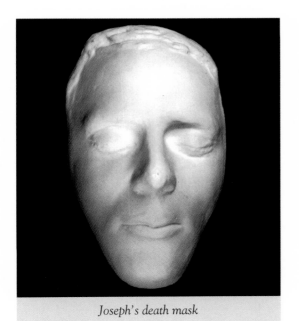

Joseph's death mask

would be interested in lending his expertise to the project. He has a deep love for Joseph Smith as well as an intense interest in the work at hand. We made arrangements to meet.

He and I spent some time examining the death masks and the photos, searching for similarities between the two forms of the brothers' images. We could see at once that the more intact skull had the same irregularity to the left side of the face that Joseph himself had. We were, at that time, unaware of the discoveries that led to the RLDS identification of the skull. Joseph's death mask confirms that he had a lower left eyebrow and cheek. The photos of the more intact skull, the RLDS Hyrum, reflect the same abnormality. Few faces are precisely symmetrical, but a difference this conspicuous is not common and did not reflect itself in what was left of the skull of the RLDS Joseph. We suddenly became aware that our research might take us beyond new and highly accurate images of Joseph and Hyrum. We were forced to begin consideration of the possibility that the bodies had been misidentified in 1928 and were buried in the wrong graves.

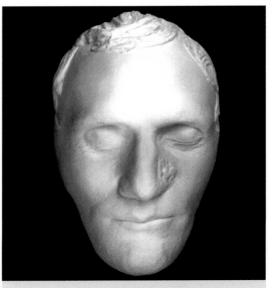

Hyrum's death mask

Next we looked at the right-side profile photo of the intact skull. It is not a perfect right angle view, although the difference is small. The skull image is actually rotated eight or nine degrees toward the camera and one or two degrees downward. This picture of the skull would provide us with an excellent view for overlaying a profile image of the death masks. If we used the computer to make comparable rotations of the masks before overlaying them, we should be able to make a crystal clear determination of which skull belonged to which brother.

RLDS Hyrum

Dr. Van De Graaff found one big problem. The jaw of the RLDS Hyrum, which was entirely separated from the skull, was not in the correct position. When photographers prepared the jaw and the skull for the pictures in 1928, an unknown object was placed on the table to raise the elevation of the skull so that the jaw could be placed under it in what observers perceived to be its correct position. But Dr. Van De Graaff pointed out that the jaw was pushed too far forward and that the base of the jaw lay flat on the table at an unnatural angle. There was only one tooth on each side of the upper jaw still in place but the joint where the back of the jawbone should go was still clearly visible in the photo. Kent believed that he could place the jaw in a nearly correct position, but he knew someone who could do a better job: Dr. Niles Herrod of Provo, Utah, an orthodontic surgeon who is also an expert in facial reconstruction.

With that observation, we decided to adjourn until we could all meet again with Dr. Herrod, if he was willing.

Meanwhile, I began the task of preparing the images in an electronic environment so that they could be controlled independently and repositioned as necessary. In earlier years, such a project would have involved making a number of exact copies of the photos, which could then be cut apart and maneuvered into an approximately correct relationship. Such an approach might be useful, although the appearance of the final arrangement often displayed evidence of the cutting and pasting, but it inherently prevented the manipulation of angles of view in the final product and could not allow for adjustments if the angles between the photos and the death masks were incompatible.

But I knew how to do it electronically and this was my expectation. During the years of my computer training I had

Dr. Van De Graaff examining skull photographs and death masks

discovered a program that would provide me with the perfect tool to move the images of these skulls into more useful positions, a program called Photoshop. Since this was just a black and white photo, I chose the Gray Scale Sharp Image format with high DPI (dots per inch) resolution, which would give me as much information as possible from the black and white image. In truth, a black-and-white image consists of thousands of shades of gray, with black and white on the ends of the monochromatic color continuum. A good photo, or for that matter even a poor one, has more shades of gray than the human eye can detect. However, in an area of a photo that seems too dark to provide any useful detail to the unaided eye, the computer can see variations and shades. By manipulating the brightness of the image and the contrasts between these shades, the computer operator can enhance details that are invisible to the naked eye.

I began at once cleaning up the photos so that the maximum amount of information would be available for the upcoming visit of the experts. I marked the dark areas of the photo that needed adjustment to a lighter shade and made the necessary

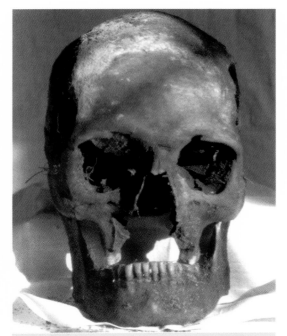

© 1993 RLDS church

RLDS Hyrum

alterations. This modification of contrast in photo images takes substantial expertise so that the modified areas do not connect with the unmodified areas with a discernable edge. Next I needed to eliminate all of the background information in the photo, any extraneous photographic data that was not part of the actual skull. I first painted a mask in the computer program of the scanned image of the photo that included just the skull, being liberal at the edges to ensure

that I did not miss even the smallest portion of the skull image. I then used program tools to magnify small portions of the masked areas so that those diminutive portions of the photo filled the entire 21-inch screen of my computer. It then became simply a matter of endurance to examine the particulars of the edges of the skull and remove any meaningless details accidentally included in the original mask.

Next I inverted the designated mask area so everything on the screen except the skull was selected. Then, by deleting the background, I left the skull uncluttered on a white background. This made the significant details of the image easier to view.

I duplicated these processes with the other photographic images of both Joseph and Hyrum. Now I had four clean skull images with out-of-place jaws.

Then I returned to the RLDS Hyrum skull. With the background portions of the image gone, I could see clearly the full outline of the jaw from front to back and from the bottom to the tip of each point of the jaw near the back of the skull. This was in fact a major stroke of luck. If the skulls and jaws had been placed in a more correct

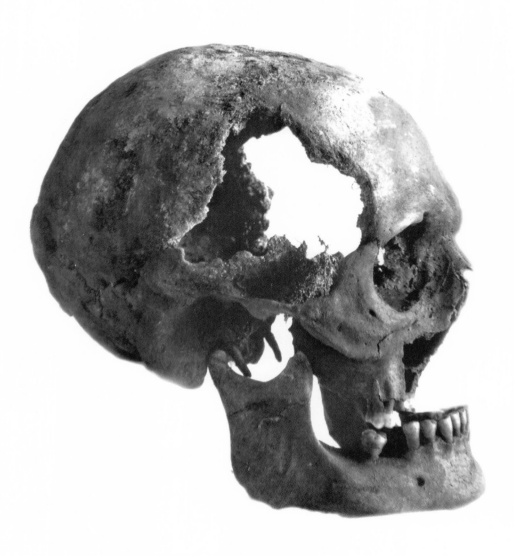

RLDS Hyrum cleaned skull photo

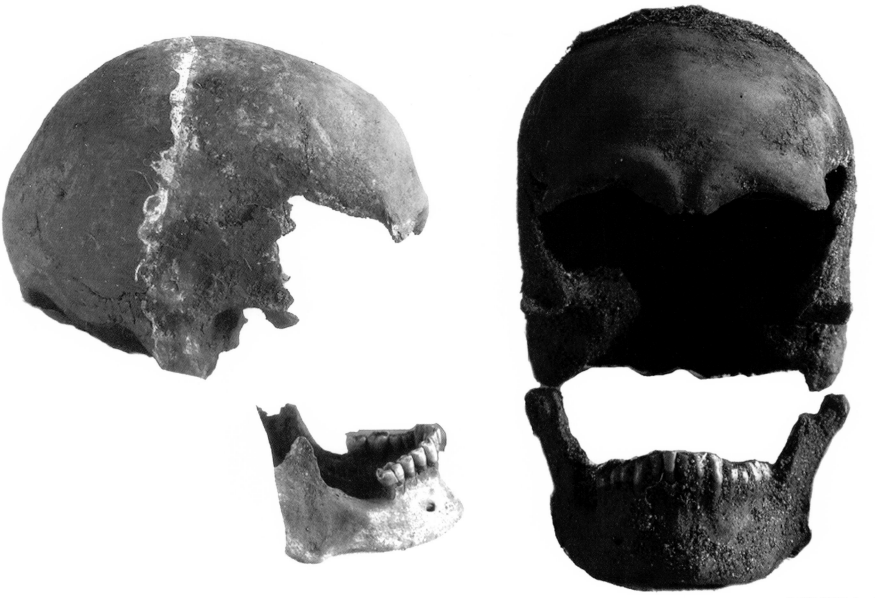

RLDS Joseph cleaned skull photo

relationship when the original photos were taken, I would have had much less information about the jaw to work with than I had now.

I carefully selected the jaw area, leaving a comfortable margin of background, as I had originally done with the entire skull, and saved the selected area as a new image of the exact size and resolution as the original. I cleaned up this new jaw image and erased the tiny remnants of the upper skull in the manner I previously described and saved the jaw image as a separate file. Then I returned to the original cleaned-up image of the full skull and removed the jaw image area from it and saved it as a new image as well. When I was finished, I had an image of the skull without the jaw and an image of the jaw without the skull.

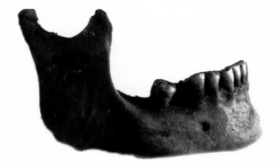

RLDS Hyrum Jaw

I repeated this routine with the side view of the other skull as well, but I left the front skull views alone. There was no point in separating the jaws and skulls of the images at this time because the adjustments needed were impossible in a 2-D environment.

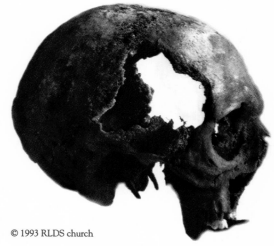

RLDS Hyrum skull

One of the remarkable capabilities of the Photoshop program is its ability to create new images by layering separate images on top of each other. This is not unlike laying multiple transparent sheets, one on top of another on an overhead projector, and projecting the entire set of images as one image onto a screen for viewing. With this Photoshop function I could paste images on top of a background without affecting the background. I could also control the opacity or color density of each layer, making it possible to see through one image to the image underneath—the opacity can be adjusted from 0% to 100%. With these capabilities, I now created an image composed of the background of the skull without the jaw and the image with the jaw on top of it. Finally, I saved the combined images in a new file and waited for the doctors to return.

This project was now burning like fire in my bones and I could hardly endure the days of delay necessary for the schedules of the two doctors to coincide so that they could come together to my office.

When they arrived, I showed them the hybrid image of the jaw and the skull. I separated the images and demonstrated how we could manipulate them and their relationship so that the jaw could be placed correctly. On the skull top we had three points of contact we could use as guides to position the jaw. The first was the socket in which the back of the jawbone would rest at the base of the skull. The second was the

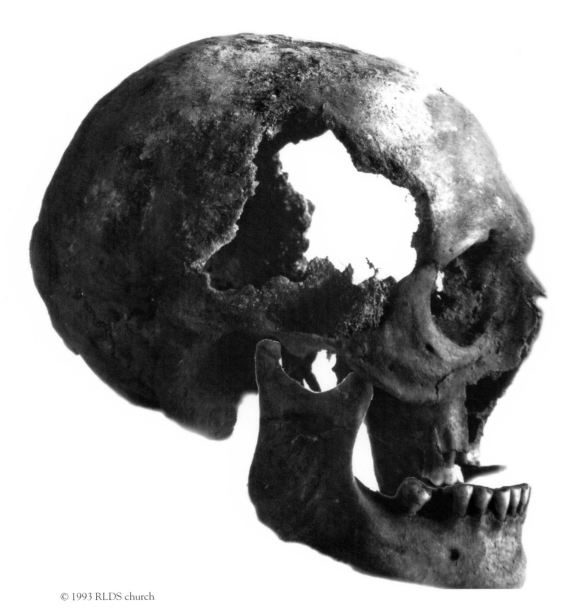

RLDS Hyrum with corrected jaw placement

place where the first point at the top of the back of the jaw would rest under the cheek bone. The last point was the remaining top molar on the right side (the left-side molar was still in place as well, but not useful from the right-angle view in the placement of the jaw) and the second bottom molar on the lower jaw. The first bottom molar on the right side was missing and appeared to have been gone long enough that the jaw-bone had healed over the space some years before death occurred. It is also possible that this molar had never developed. As we looked at these teeth, we discovered that an unusual wear pattern on the top molar looked like it could match up with a corre-sponding pattern on the lower second molar, which had clearly rotated forward to fill part of the gap made in the jaw by the missing first molar. Using these three points we could position the jaw within a couple of millimeters of its correct location on the skull. We rotated and moved and adjusted the placement of the jaw until the points of contact aligned perfectly and the jaw seemed to repose in a correct and restful state.

When we were finished, Dr. Herrod was so certain of the evidence of the contact points and wear patterns that he wrote: "It is with absolute confidence that the RLDS Hyrum skull and mandible are appropriately aligned as evidenced by the appropriate wear faceting of the articulated tooth."[85]

The final image was startling. The face we saw did not have the weak jaw indicated by the death mask of Joseph, but neither did it look like the profile of Hyrum.

We now had a front profile, complete and with correct jaw placement of the RLDS Hyrum. But whose image was it in reality? According to the record from the RLDS excavation, it was Hyrum's, but this likeness did not seem to match up at all with the visible evidence from the death masks.

We then looked at the other skull and jaw and very quickly came to the conclusion that too little remained of the top of the skull to allow us to place the jaw in any similar fashion. We determined to concentrate on the intact skull and match the death masks to it by process of elimination. If we could make a positive identification of one, we would then know the identity of the other, assuming that they are in fact the skulls of the brothers.

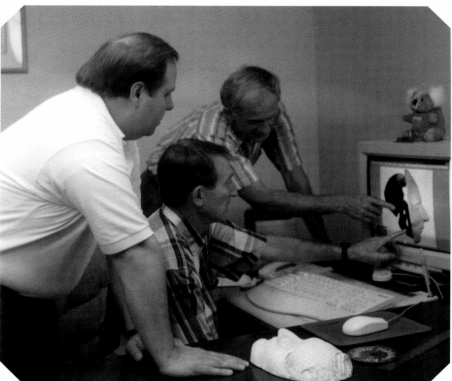

Shannon Tracy, Dr. Niles Herrod, and Dr. Kent Van De Graaff examining the RLDS Hyrum photograph in prepartion for proper jaw placement

We then, after matching the correct death mask with the more intact skull, could match the remaining death mask with the other skull and align the jaw to the death mask in a reverse procedure of the sequence followed with the first skull.

Our intent was to identify the skulls conclusively. To do this we would need to match up the information of which we were certain with some partially known and sometimes inconclusive information. In this case, the proven information related to the identity of those from whose features the death masks were fashioned. We know which death mask is from the face of Joseph and which one is from the face of Hyrum. These identifications have never been challenged. We also know that the skulls belong to Hyrum and Joseph, even though in our minds there was now some doubt about which skull belonged to which brother. After some discussion about what needed to be done, the doctors departed and I began the technical work of identification.

Several observations assisted me as I began this phase of the investigation. I knew that Hyrum was shot twice in the head. One ball entered his skull at the left side of his nose. The other ball grazed the right side of his chest while he lay on the floor, entering under his jaw at the top of his neck. The first shot is verified by the death mask and the eyewitness report of Willard Richards. For the other shots we have only the written report of the Huntingtons concerning the wounds they found when they cleaned the bodies and evidence of a grazing shot to the right breast as seen on Hyrum's clothes. Joseph had no

Location of the wounds on Hyrum's body as indicated by the stars: left side of face; under jaw; grazed right chest; back right, through kidney; right side hip; left knee

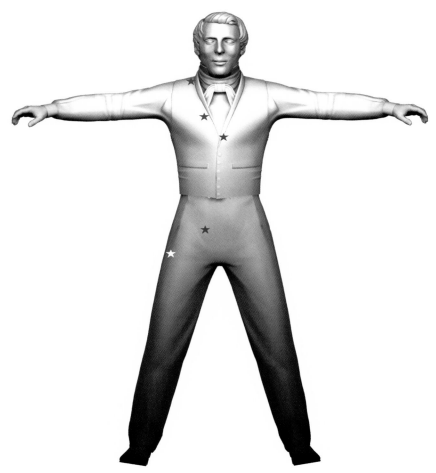

Location of the wounds on Joseph's body as indicated by the stars: right collarbone; right chest; below heart; lower bowels; back side, right hip

shots to the head, only to the body. Two reports cited earlier in this book indicate that he may have been struck in the face with a pewter fife after falling to the ground from the window of his cell.[86]

The incomplete skull, the RLDS Joseph, clearly implies massive head trauma by the extent of the missing areas in the front of the skull and at the base. The shot to the face would easily account for the missing facial bones and the second shot would account for the lack of bone in the base of the skull. The intact skull has only the upper jaw back to the first molars missing and a small piece of bone missing from the right side of the nasal area. This upper facial abnormality could have been caused by blunt trauma to the face after death or from the excavation. Fractured bone will of course deteriorate more quickly and would have a higher probability of disintegration after the deterioration of the connective tissue. I need to point out that the manner in which the bodies were found was not a careful archaeological dig. Many of the bone fragments that are missing from the two skulls in all likelihood are still there in the gravesite, overlooked by men

untrained in the work they were doing. Teeth are always slow to decay. Therefore most or all of the missing teeth of both skulls should still have been present at the site. But they were never located. The records do not suggest that anyone even thought to look for them or any other unattached fragments of the skeletons. At least I did not see in the written reports any evidence of sifting the ground for missing bone matter. Also the break in the right cheek of the more intact skull has the appearance of being fresh. The edges are

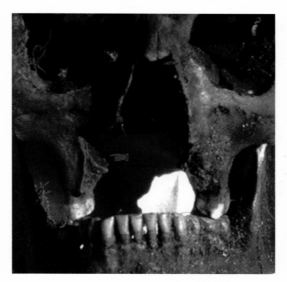

Note the sharp break lines of the upper jaw. The normal deterioration of the skull has not rounded the edges as elsewhere evident on the skull.

sharp and there is no sign of erosion as in other areas on the same skull that have deteriorated over the years. It is at least possible that this part of the facial trauma of the RLDS Hyrum occurred during the process of excavation.

With these observations I elected to begin my efforts to verify the identities of the skulls with the comparison of Joseph's death mask to the more intact skull, the RLDS Hyrum. To make this correlation, I needed a clean side profile of the death mask in the computer to scale and rotate as we had done with the lower jawbone. I have a friend who has access to a Beta SP video camera and light table. He hooked the video output of the camera to the input of a high-end digital video card in my computer system, thus enabling us to convey any images we desired from the camera directly into the computer. We placed the masks on a black background on the light table with the camera mounted overhead. Then we made right-side profiles and frontal shots of each mask and stored these as computer images.

Now I was ready. I loaded the combined image of the skull and the correctly placed jaw and prepared to overlay the image of Joseph's death mask. I had previously used a photographic image of the mask to make a side profile of the death mask on a white background. I had arrived at a point where I could at last examine factual data and make verifiable conclusions from observable evidence.

I opened up the hybrid image of the skull and jaw and created a new layer to receive the death mask and pasted it into that layer. I had to work with the scale of the death mask so that it would correspond to the size of the skull images. The software I used allowed me to maintain exact ratios as I moved the scale up and down. I was thus able to keep the image in a correct aspect ratio to the original image as I worked with it.

My first discovery was that Joseph's death mask needed to be tilted back more at the top. Joseph had a high, sloping forehead. In order to capture the full facial features, George Cannon apparently tilted the plaster cast down at the top of the head to cover the full detail. This would explain why Joseph's mask makes his chin look weak and recessed when the mask is laid flat

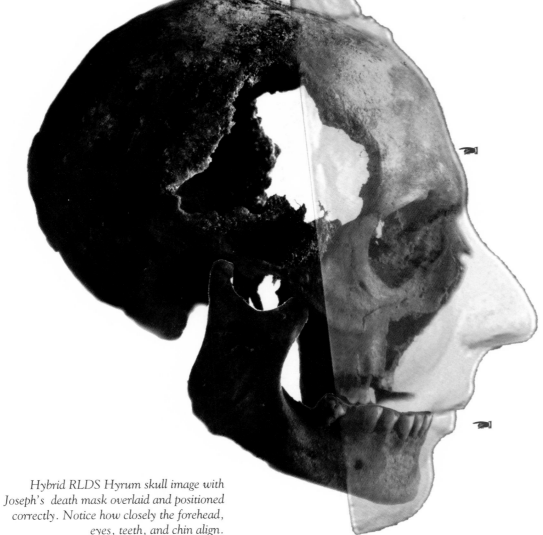

Hybrid RLDS Hyrum skull image with Joseph's death mask overlaid and positioned correctly. Notice how closely the forehead, eyes, teeth, and chin align.

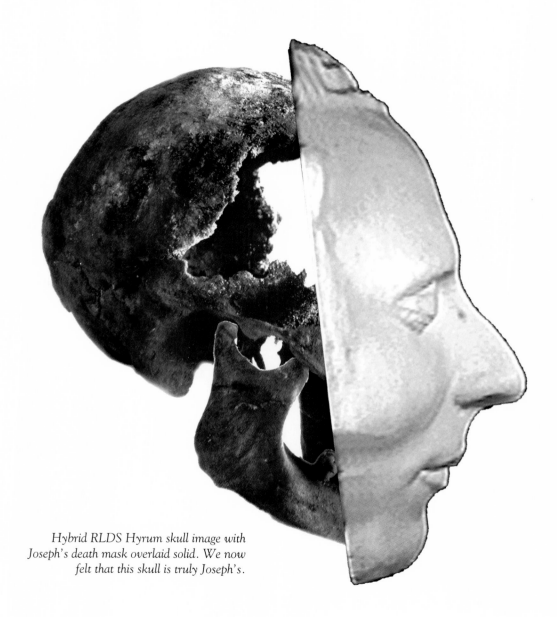

Hybrid RLDS Hyrum skull image with Joseph's death mask overlaid solid. We now felt that this skull is truly Joseph's.

on a table. When Joseph's mask is compared to Hyrum's, it is immediately clear that they were not cast at the same angle. Joseph's mask must be rotated upward at the bottom to be in the same plane as Hyrum's. I needed to rotate the image of Joseph's mask out at the bottom and back at the top to correct this discrepancy.

I made the necessary adjustments of rotation and scale and moved the transparent image of Joseph's death mask over the image of the skull and jaw. They matched perfectly! The death mask lined up at almost every location of the front skull profile. In fact, the only adjustment needed was caused by eight-degree rotation of the skull photo from a perfect right angle. Once that was corrected, I had no doubts. This skull (the one the RLDS officers had identified as Hyrum's) belonged to Joseph's death mask.

The likeness itself was striking. I was looking at an image of Joseph based on physiological data never before used in examining his appearance. I believe this image to be more accurate than anyone had seen in over 150 years.

I wasn't finished yet. Much would yet need to be done to prepare and present

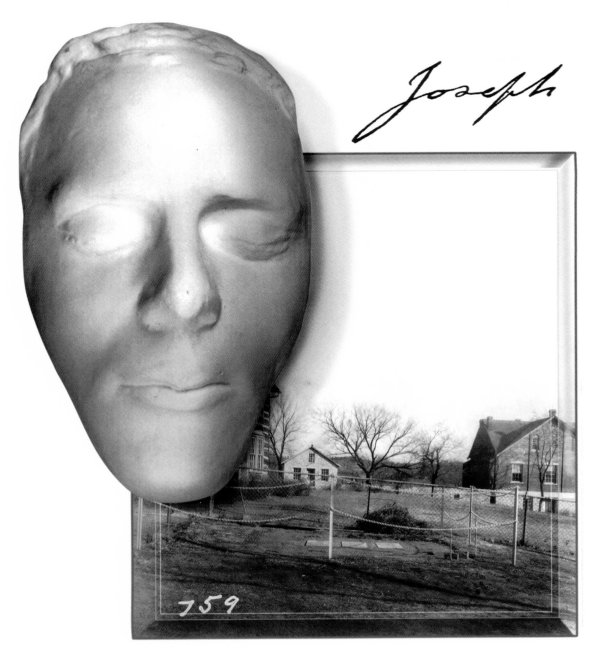

Joseph

to the world an image of Joseph that was accurate in *every* respect. But I could see him before me now, on the screen of my computer, and I knew that we were going to have enough information to complete the work and allow people to see Joseph with more accuracy than he had been seen since 1844.

I looked around in my office and found myself alone—it was early in the morning by then. I wanted to celebrate but had no one to celebrate with. I looked at the phone, but the hour was late. This moment was mine alone. Later I would tell others, but for now, the wonder and the reverence belonged to me.

CHAPTER 9

Putting It All Together

was eager to show the combined image to Dr. Van De Graaff and Dr. Herrod. I believed that their input would verify the accuracy of what I was certain I was now seeing. I also needed help to fine-tune the image with any additional adjustments that might be needed. When Dr. Van De Graaff returned to my office, he concurred with my conclusions in every respect. Our inescapable judgment was that the RLDS Hyrum skull did in fact belong to Joseph. Dr. Van De Graaff suggested some adjustments, but the evidence was compelling. Within a cement slab on the property of the Homestead in Nauvoo, Illinois, two brothers were buried, but our conclusion was that the names above did not match the location of the remains below.

We invested some time in examination of the other skull and determined that it would present a much greater challenge to match with the death mask in the same manner. The less intact skull (the RLDS Joseph that we now were certain belonged to Hyrum) had a double rotation differential. The top of the skull was rotated nine degrees toward the camera but the jaw was rotated away from the camera. This image would never allow for as clean an overlay as the first one in a two-dimensional (2-D) computer environment. After long discussion and many attempts, we admitted that we had reached the limits of our ability and technology. What we wanted to accomplish we could not accomplish while working in the two-dimensional environment of Photoshop.

The time had come to digitize the death masks.

For final construction of the images of Joseph and Hyrum, the images I hoped to make, we would want to unite the masks and skulls

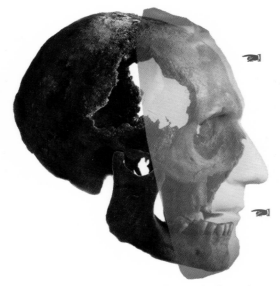

RLDS Hyrum skull with Hyrum death mask overlay. Note how the forehead pulls away and the teeth and chin are out of place.

in a 3-D environment in the computer. When we were ready, we could overlay the digitized masks with the photo images of the skulls, matching the rotations and aligning the two together with an accuracy impossible in 2-D space.

Digitization is a process that collects points in space and links them with lines, creating a wire frame or mesh that defines the physical structure of an object. The digitization process converts the grid on a model into 3-D geometry within the computer. With a model of a human form, the lines must be laid down to follow natural contours and curves and will not generally intersect at right angles. The intersection of lines will form geometric figures which will be input into the computer with an electronic stylus.

By uniting the images of the masks with the photos of the skulls in 3-D space, we would have a much more effective environment for final confirmation of the identity of the less intact skull. A more accurate conformation of the more intact skull would also be found there.

The time had arrived for my first meeting with Chris Creek and his remarkable associates. Their business, Zygote Media Group, had agreed to provide the necessary hardware and software for the digitizing of the death masks and for other related projects. I had my first meeting with Chris and his assistants at his office in Mapleton, Utah. We sat around a small, low, round table and discussed the order in which things ought to happen. First, a detailed grid pattern needed to be drawn onto the masks themselves. It may be helpful to think of this grid pattern as a

Initial meeting with Chris Creek and the crew: Chris Creek, Roger Clarke, Shannon Tracy, Dr. Kent Van De Graaff

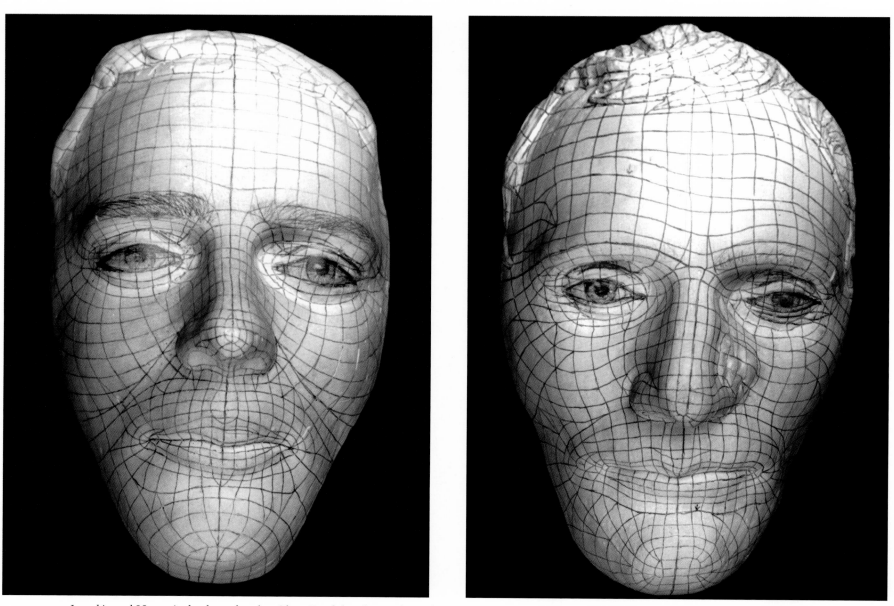

Joseph's and Hyrum's death masks after Chris Creek has drawn the grid onto the faces. Notice that the lines follow the natural contours of the masks.

series of contour lines such as you would see on a topographical map. These lines would, however, be drawn on real 3-D images rather than on two-dimensional documents. No great skill is required to draw lines on models, but it takes a true expert to draw them in a manner that lets the operator capture the most amount of information from a model. As the grid pattern is created, it is important to follow natural body lines and curves. If too much space occurs between lines, the elevation of the features, that is the differences in the height

Eric Merritt at 3-D digitizing station inputting point coordinates from Joseph's gridded death mask

between points on the image, will not be accurately recorded. As the lines are applied and recorded, the grid is defined. At times it may be necessary to go back and add more lines to a particular area to better define its physical properties.

Once the operator is satisfied with the amount of detail that is defined in the grids, the model is then ready to digitize. Chris is one of only a handful of experts in this field who can look at a model and know where best to place lines and define the grid to maximize information for human form reproduction in three dimensions. He would be the one to define our masks. He assured us that the time we spent in becoming familiar with the death masks would help us, and talking in advance about the features found there would prove valuable to the gridding process.

When we began to digitize the masks, the operator selected a quadrilateral (a four-sided, irregular geometric figure) on the mask. He then placed the tip of the stylus on one of the corners and selected it. That point was then stored in the memory of the computer at a location based upon its real world location reference to an image

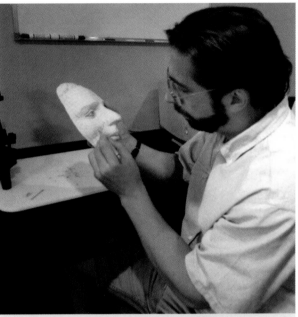

Chris Creek laying out grid pattern on Joseph's death mask

center point established by the digitizer. The operator then proceeded to work the stylus around the other corners of the quadrilateral, selecting and marking them until all four were defined. The computer then connected the points with a line established in 3-D space—a line that indicated the location of each point as being up, down, left, right, in, or out from the previous point. Slowly the image of the model was transferred to 3-D space in the computer.

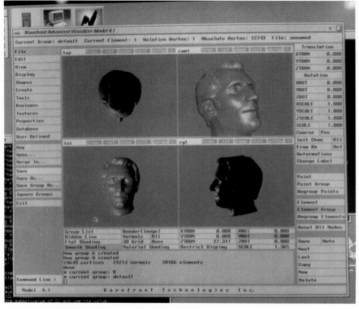

Left: Hyrum's 3-D model in quad view in N-geometry

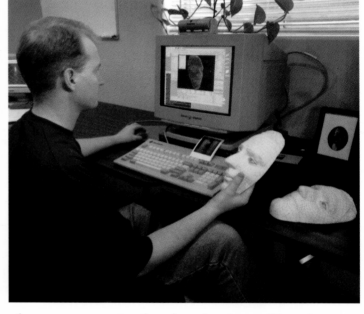

Right: Roger adding detail to the face of Joseph in N-geometry, checking location on the line-mapped death mask

As a model is being defined in the computer, it sometimes becomes necessary to rotate or change the position of the image to facilitate the input of other points. To do this it is necessary to establish common points of reference that the computer can use in its new position and its former location. Those who practice orienteering use similar methods to keep from becoming disoriented or lost. Participants who are about to change locations might select a mountain peak or other unusual geologic formation as a reference point that can be readily identified when they arrive at

a new location. So it is in the process of digitization. Once the object is moved, the common points are reselected and the computer is ready to continue its imaging process.

The experience of watching the images of Joseph and Hyrum materialize on the computer screen was powerful. Each new piece of geometric information, each new line and each new curve moved us closer to a final portrait.

After both masks were digitized, the photographs of the skulls were digitized also and precise outlines established of the infor-

mation found on the photos. These line tracings represent the outline of the skulls in space at their given rotation from the camera. Since these are 2-D images, they show distance from the lens by a decrease in size. This fact is critical to remember when building the models. Reference points found in the line traces can be measured and compared only when the model is rotated in the same degree of rotation from the camera as was the original object at the time the photograph was taken.

The skulls photos presented interesting challenges as we labored to convert them into a useful format in the computer. They are two-dimensional images, with depth indicated by lights and shadows, and distance indicated by size. Thus, the portions of the mask farthest from the camera are smaller than the sections closest to the lens. This photographic effect, called *foreshortening*, together with the rotations of the masks from precise right angles, made the marriage of the masks and the skulls the sort of achievement that could be accomplished *only* in the computer. Computer capabilities enable skilled workers to rotate images by degrees to the left and to the right, and also

up and down. If someone tried to lay an image taken at a true ninety-degree angle over one that had a rotation of eight degrees toward the camera, the images would not match correctly. The only way to test two images for correct alignment is to match the degree of rotation from the camera.

To do this with our images, we placed the trace of the skulls and the photos of the skulls at a true ninety degree angle (from our viewpoint) in the computer, thus ensuring that our placement of the images did not compound the problems caused by the minor rotations in the original photos.

Then we brought the 3-D image of the death masks and rotated them eight degrees toward the camera, so that they had the same rotation that the skulls originally had from the lens of the camera at the time the photos were taken. Once the death masks were digitized, they could be scaled, moved, or rotated until they lined up with the front of the skull images or until the lack of a relationship proved that there was no match. Because the images of the skulls were originally turned eight degrees toward the camera, the death masks also needed to be rotated the same eight degrees. Then we

Left: Roger Clarke working on the digitized death mask and the photo of the skull in 3-D

Right: *Joseph's 3-D death mask superimposed over traced outline of the skull in the N-geometry program*

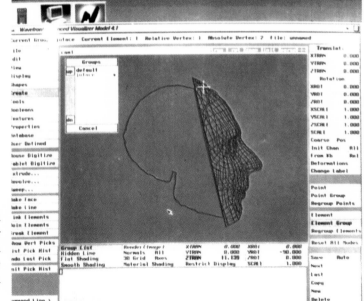

could overlay the masks on the skulls and determine if there was a correlation of the death masks and the photos of the skulls. By this process we were able to show exactly how the more intact skull photo matched the Joseph Smith death mask. Overlays that do not concede this necessary correction between images would not have allowed us to match the profiles created by the eight-degree rotation when the photos were taken. On the more intact skull, this rotation makes part of the front left side of the skull visible. This would clearly cause an incorrect profile for any ninety-degree overlays.

To illustrate, note that the flat part of the forehead does not make any gross changes in angle, but the eyebrow area clearly does, and this change will grossly exaggerate the change in that area from the eyebrow to the bridge of the nose. This is a mistake many have made. All those who have created 2-D images of the Prophet based on other 2-D images have apparently failed to see the importance of rotation and foreshortening.

With the images corrected for rotations and distance distortions, we were able to

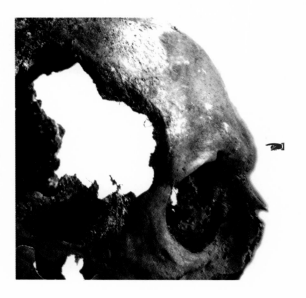

Above: Note the brow area of the skull. Part of the left side is showing because of the eight-degree rotation of the skull in the photo.

Below: Hyrum's 3-D wire frame death mask is aligned with the 3-D Hyrum model.

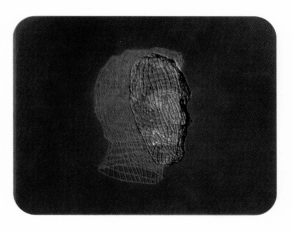

show that the more intact skull photo matched the Joseph Smith death mask exactly.

By proper rotation and adjustment, we were also able to show how well the less intact skull matched up to Hyrum's death mask in our 3-D environment. As mentioned above, the less intact skull had both a rotation and perspective problem. To make the comparison, we were required to rotate the Hyrum death mask nine degrees toward the camera. We then placed the top of the skull forehead area and the top of the mask area together. They matched with a startling precision. We locked these two objects together and then rotated them until we could match the jaw up with the mask. This type of observation would be very difficult to make without a computer. The nature of linear restrictions, the need for exact rotations, the matching of angles, and locking of objects together in any other medium or environment would be almost impossible. Even if it could be done, the resulting achievement would lack the precision and smoothness seen in these images.

Although the process in which I was involved with Chris Creek and his crew involves significantly more detail, I have tried to provide enough detail to help the reader understand the exactness of the requirements we imposed on all of our work. Others have tried to match information from the artist's tracings of the photos without using a computer, but have encountered tremendous difficulties in maintaining accuracy. For the level of precision we sought, the thickness of a pencil line would be too much variance and well outside our acceptable tolerances.

When the work with the Hyrum death mask was completed, we felt as though we had reached a significant plateau in our work. If our work could be compared to the building of a home, then we had laid the foundation and finished the framing. The drywall was up and the plumbing and electrical systems were in place. Now it was time for the detail work: the molding and painting and carpeting. Now it was time for the finishing touches.

"The Ends of the Earth Shall Inquire after Thy Name"

e moved computer files of the matched and locked objects into a third program, into an environment called N-geometry, where we could finish the detail and sculpturing of the heads based upon skeletal details corrected for foreshortening, rotation, and death mask information.

For the portions of the images where there was no information available, careful coaching by Dr. Van De Graaff in rules of anatomy enabled us to fill in the gaps. The digitized death masks combined with the skull photos gave us an immense amount of information, much more than anyone could have derived from the physical descriptions alone. And since the photos and masks gave us so much knowledge, we could fill in the gaps in our knowledge with a high degree of certainty.

Once the models were brought into the N-geometry environment, the detailing and modeling could be finished. Hours of study of the death masks and the photos were needed to check and recheck the images of the models. Details impossible to derive from the digitization process were reintroduced to the models by physically matching their location on the gridded death mask and creating them again on the 3-D model in the same area of the grid. Wrinkles and lip definition were added with this procedure. We periodically used the computer to place the original death mask images over the models to determine if we had strayed in any way from the original. There were some details that needed correction because of death and of the physical trauma that occurred before death. Hyrum's nose had to be put back in the correct position. It was displaced to the right and upward a bit by the ball that struck his face. The skin above this facial wound was compressed upward when the area of

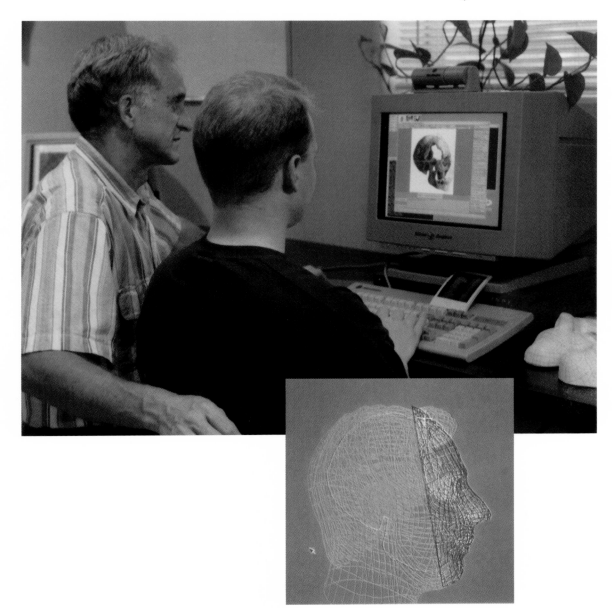

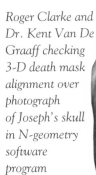

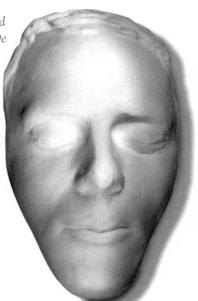

Roger Clarke and Dr. Kent Van De Graaff checking 3-D death mask alignment over photograph of Joseph's skull in N-geometry software program

Joseph's 3-D wire frame death mask superimposed over the outline tracing of the skull photograph and 3-D model

the wound was filled with cotton soaked in camphor.

We opened the eye sockets on the new models. We placed correct eyes within with separate whites of the eyes, irises, and pupils so that we could have full eye detail. We also separated the lips and built the insides of the mouths, including teeth, gums, and even a tongue, so that later we could have the brothers smile and even speak. The eyebrows are not well defined on the mask and were probably matted down with grease. For those, we made separate objects of approximate shape and size that could later be given the qualities of hair. We even opened up the nostrils so that correct shadows would be made around the nose. The ears were made based upon the collection of images that we had of the brothers, including drawings, oils, and sculptures. The hair was actually sculpted in clay on the head of a model and then digitized into the computer and adjusted to fit the likenesses of Joseph and Hyrum.

Several measurements were taken of the skulls in 1928 while they were in the Mansion House being photographed, and the numbers were preserved. One of the photos shows a ruler and offers some size comparison and, perhaps, evidence of the tool used for the measurements, although this is never specified in the reports. People learning of the measurements might be inclined to declare, "Here are some hard facts. Why haven't you used them? These numbers are hard data taken from the very skulls."

Nothing would have pleased me more than to have been able to use these measurements. But some questions associated with them simply have no answers. For example, what device was used to make the measurements? Was it the old wooden ruler pictured in some of the photos of the backs of the skulls? Or were calipers employed? Perhaps a tape measure? It is important to know which. If calipers were used, then the readings could be precise, although they would still have required frequent calibration. Any other instrument would introduce at

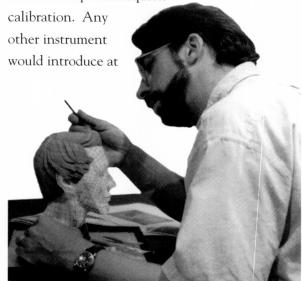

Chris Creek modeling hair in clay

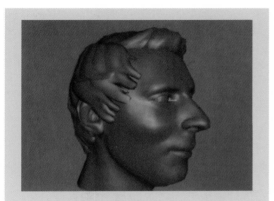

Above: Model of Joseph as seen in the N-geometry program

Top right: Joseph's 3-D model in quad view as seen in N-geometry

Lower right: Chris Creek and the crew (Roger Clarke, Chris Creek, Eric Merritt)

least an element of subjectivity. But there is a more important deficiency in these dimensions. We have no indication of the exact points of the beginning and ending of each skull measurement. Since there are no marked places on the skull photos, and since beginning and ending points of the various measurements were never precisely specified, a tremendous amount of error can be expected. For this information to be useful, markers should have been placed on the skulls at each location of the starting and ending points and these points then photographed to record the exact places so that others could find the same locations on the skulls today. And of course the photographers and church officials working in the Mansion House with the skeletal remnants of the Martyrs had no idea of the use to which their images would be put. But the numbers are tantalizing. If those who made the measurements and recorded the numbers had been more meticulous in their notations

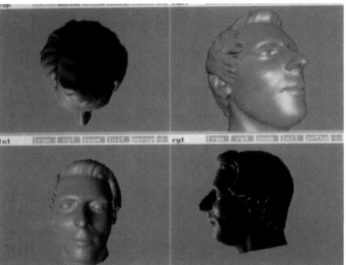

and examinations, this data would be of inestimable value.

Some have used these calculations in preparing images of Joseph and Hyrum,

assuming that the existence of these numbers is evidence of care and accuracy and precision. But when we considered them against the background of the accuracy of the identification of the remains of the Martyrs, and other events associated with the exhumation and reinternment, our confidence wavered. Nevertheless, we looked at these numbers over and over again, hoping to find useful facts. We could not.

The death masks are unrefuted facts. We have based our work on these and accepted as useful and factual only the information that agreed with them. We have used them as a foundation for the re-creation of the images of the Prophet and the Patriarch. Where specific information has been unavailable, we have followed anatomical guidelines for muscle, skin, and spacing. Thus we are sure that the images are as correct as it was possible for us to make them.

Our research led us to some interesting discoveries about things we had not anticipated. We found that Joseph probably ground his teeth. This fact is suggested by the wear patterns evident on the teeth still attached to his skull. The doctors also concluded that he might have suffered from some amount of gum disease.

Joseph was missing the first molar on the bottom right side. Some time in his life he may have suffered a severe blow to the left cheek and eye area, causing the bones to be broken. Left untreated, such an injury might have mended in a slightly abnormal position, lower and back a bit, resulting in the facial asymmetry we observed in both the skull and the mask. Joseph had a smaller-than-usual occipital lobe area which made the lower portion of the back of his head small in proportion to the rest of his head. This would tend to make his face seem more prominent from a side view.

Hyrum had prominent brow features which are evident from the death mask and confirmed by the photos of his skull.

I have been concerned, as I have applied minute and exacting scientific empiricism to the features of these men, that some who love and follow them might take offense, as though we had spattered mud on the Mona Lisa, or painted graffiti on the sculptures of Mount Rushmore. I hope no one has felt or will feel this way. The mortality and humanity of Joseph and Hyrum Smith have made this study possible. The evidence here discussed has demonstrated that Joseph and Hyrum Smith were men, with the physical frailties and susceptibilities of men. If they were not physically perfect in every respect, they were spiritually extraordinary. They were prophets, seers, and revelators, called of God to do a great work. If their bodies had imperfections, their spirits did not. God knew them and loved them and called them.

We visited Eldred G. Smith, Patriarch Emeritus to The Church of Jesus Christ of Latter-day Saints and great great grandson of the Patriarch Hyrum, to examine the clothes of Hyrum and to see the other personal items that had belonged to him. While there, we took careful measurements of the clothing Hyrum was wearing in the Carthage Jail. We made video and photographic records so that we could use this information in building complete body images, including clothing, for both brothers. We took great care with this examination. We measured every possible dimension of the clothing including even the size of buttons and the distance between button-

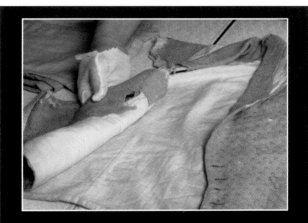

Hyrum's vest showing the elongated path of the bullet in the right side

LDS Patriarch Emeritus Eldred G. Smith displaying Hyrum's trousers, worn at the time of the Martyrdom, and pointing out the bullet hole

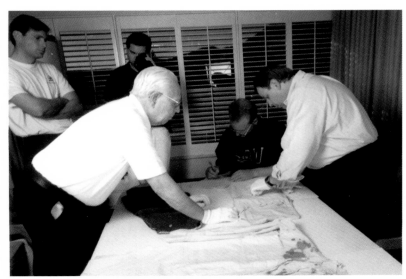

Patriarch Smith, Roger Clarke, and Shannon Tracy taking measurements of Hyrum's shirt and vest

Hyrum's shirt with bloodstains on the right side

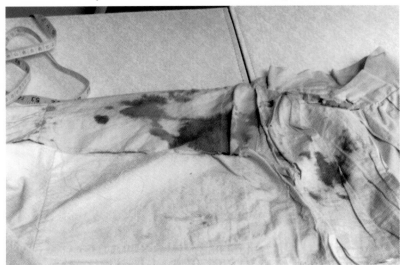

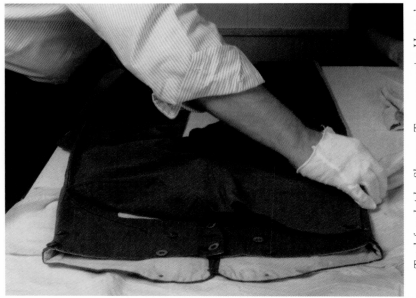

Top left and right: Shannon Tracy measuring Hyrum's trousers and vest

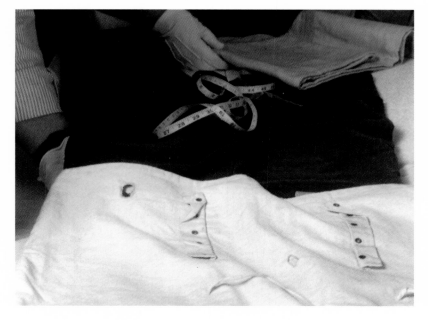

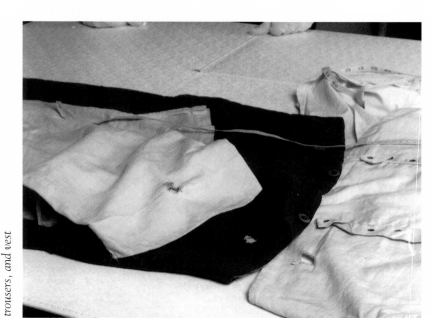

Bottom left and right: The back of Hyrum's clothing. Note how the bullet holes align through the undergarment, trousers, and vest

Hyrum's sunglasses; note the side panels of glass which pull out to offer protection from sunglare from the side. Hyrum left his good watch (center) at his home in Nauvoo when he went to Carthage. His everyday watch (right) was shattered by the bullet that passed through his back.

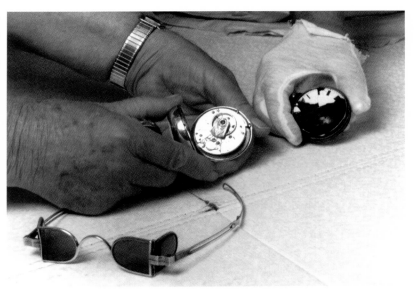

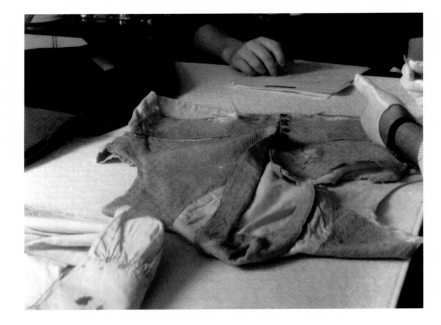

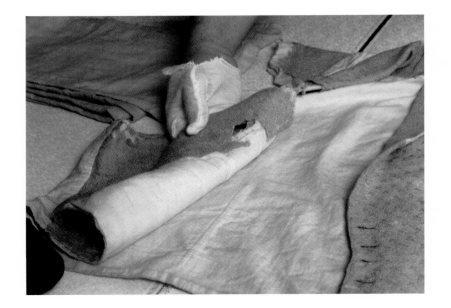

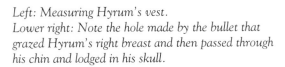

Left: Measuring Hyrum's vest.
Lower right: Note the hole made by the bullet that grazed Hyrum's right breast and then passed through his chin and lodged in his skull.

holes. We knew that the clothes would give us an important indication about Hyrum's size as well as a useful model for the kind of clothing that might have been worn by Joseph. We have assumed that the clothing is precise in both cut and fit. Hyrum's vest was of a unique pattern of silk weave and his buttons were of bone. The vest was laced in the back, no doubt to give a better body fit. Hyrum's trousers had a front flap that buttoned up on either side. The flap could be buttoned at the top or one or both corners could be folded down and buttoned at an angle. The shirt had very fine stitching at all seams and was gathered at the cuffs, which were held together by links.

Joseph and Hyrum both weighed about the same amount, around two hundred pounds. But Joseph was shorter, and the difference in height would have made Joseph more stocky. We have no clear statements or data on the width of the bodies. Our renditions of this feature would have to be subjective, determined by paintings and basic anatomical relationships.

Other items that were shown to us were Hyrum's watches and his sunglasses. We

were shown his good watch that he left at home when he went to Carthage and the one that was broken by impact of the ball that entered his back. This watch was in his

Alvin's wooden toolbox that Joseph borrowed to temporarily house the gold plates

front vest pocket. His sunglasses were of high quality and had panels that folded out to block sun coming in from the side. Eldred G. Smith also showed us Hyrum's sword and rifle from the Nauvoo Legion, and we also saw Joseph Smith Senior's school bell.

But to me the most interesting item was Alvin's toolbox that Hyrum sent to Joseph the night the Prophet was finally given the gold plates by Moroni. It was to be the first storage recepticle of the plates until other arrangements could be made. This very box held plates that were handled and inscribed by Nephi, Jacob, Mormon, and Moroni. This wooden artifact was a connection for us with times past and with events of great magnitude. I was humbled. I am very grateful to Patriarch Smith for the time he took and the special viewing he allowed us. He has been a great help in our project.

With this collected information we were now prepared to complete and clothe the entire physical structure of our models.

The process was time consuming but straightforward. The days and weeks raced by. I was observing the development of a creation of unprecedented significance. I cannot describe the feelings of wonder and love that filled me as I watched the faces of these remarkable men begin to materialize before me. I have always loved Joseph and Hyrum. But now, as this extraordinary journey, this search for Joseph, began to spiral toward its conclusion, I felt something more. My immersion in his life, in his death, in his form and features had somehow immersed me in his soul. What I now felt was love, of course, but love multiplied by the flame of a testimony whose heat I could feel in my very cells, a testimony that has changed my life.

I knew two exceedingly important things as I made the final adjustments that would enable me to view the completed images of the Prophet and his brother. I knew that I would soon see exactly what they looked like, and I knew that what they looked like did not matter. Compared to the eternal majesty of Joseph Smith's work, his appearance has little significance.

Do not suppose, as I offer this confession, that I am apologizing for what I have done, for my search for Joseph's face has brought me closer than I had ever hoped to his heart. My deepest prayer is that somehow, someone, seeing what I have been permitted to do, will have that same experience.

Final 3-D camera view of Joseph Smith

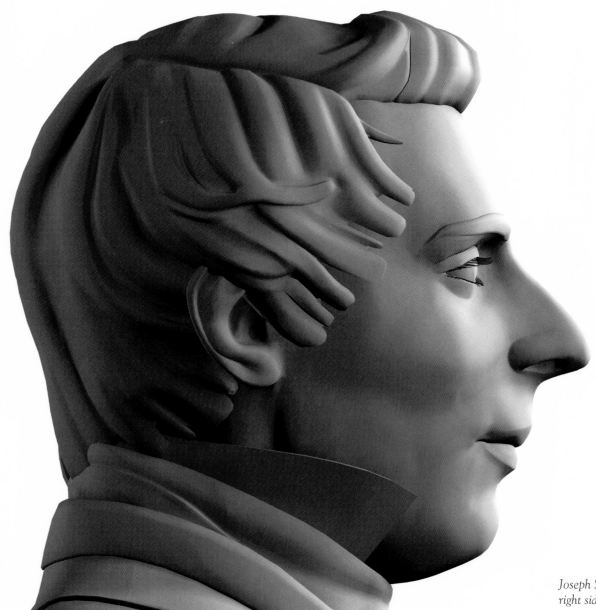

Joseph Smith 3-D computer image,
right side

Joseph Smith 3-D computer image,
left side

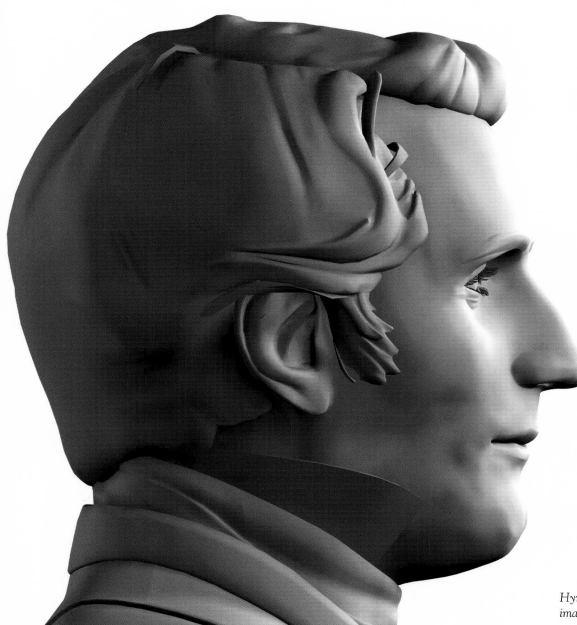

Hyrum Smith 3-D computer image, right side

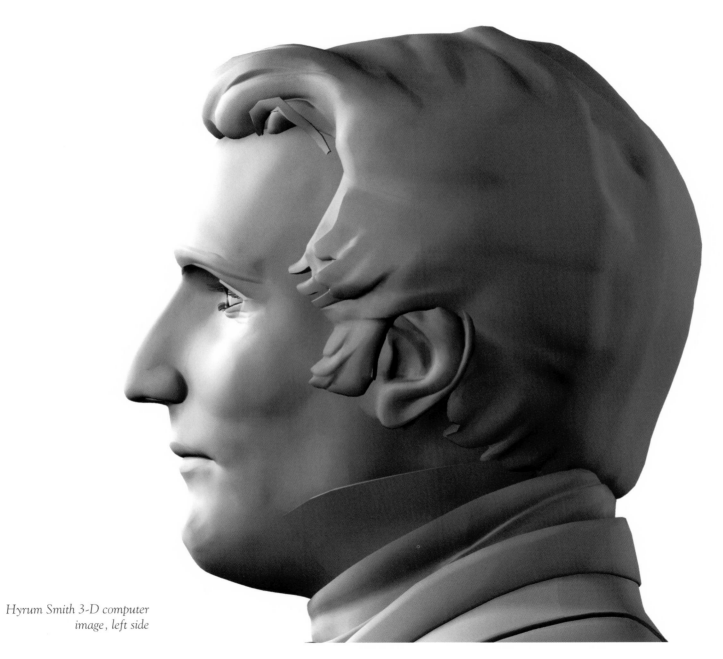

*Hyrum Smith 3-D computer
image, left side*

Joseph front computer image

Hyrum front computer image

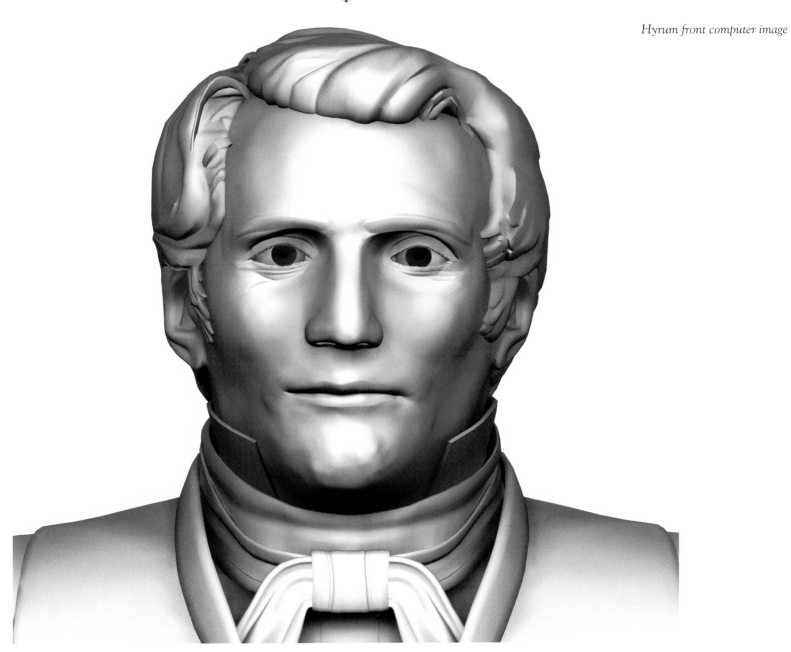

Joseph full body computer model. Clothing is modeled after the clothing Hyrum was wearing at Carthage.

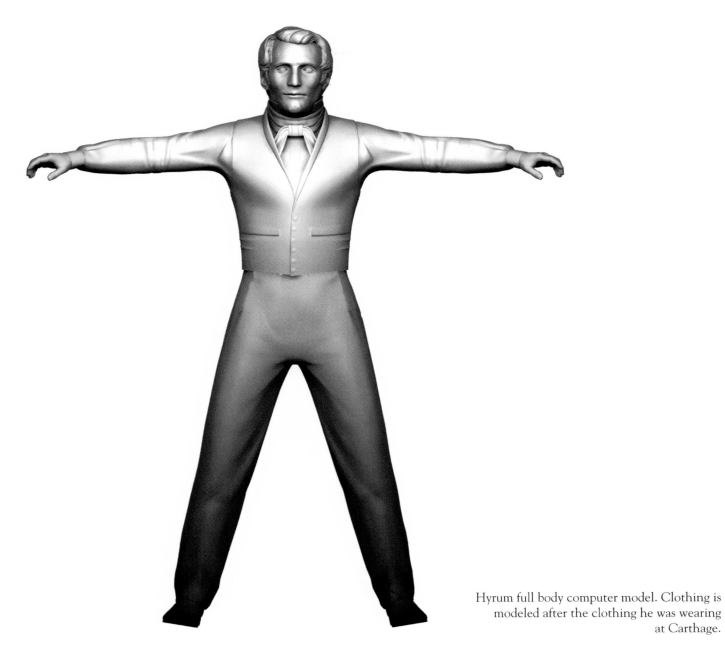

Hyrum full body computer model. Clothing is modeled after the clothing he was wearing at Carthage.

Joseph full body computer model,
left and right sides

Hyrum full body computer model,
left and right sides

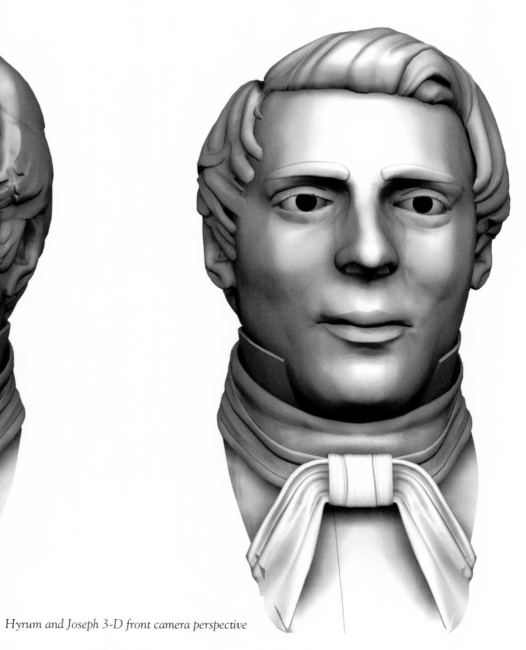

Hyrum and Joseph 3-D front camera perspective

A Maudsley drawing of Joseph overlaid with the 3-D model, the skull, and the death mask. Notice how closely the Maudsley front profile matches the other elements.

Joseph Smith 3-D camera front perspective